Nuremberg and Beyond

The Memoirs of Siegfried Ramler

From 20th Century Europe to Hawai'i

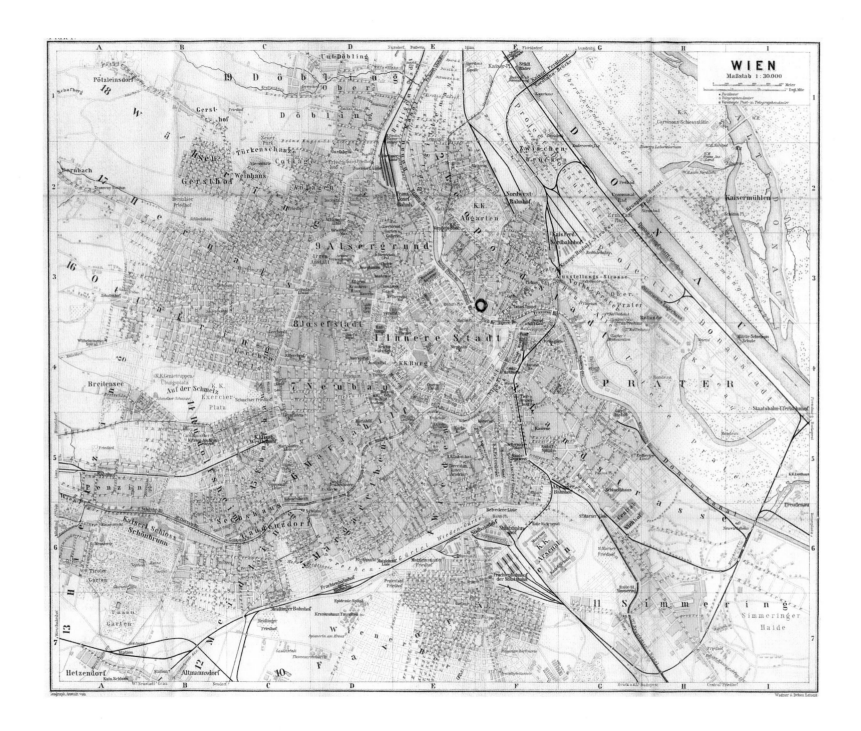

WIEN
Maßstab 1 : 30.000

Geograph. Anstalt von

Wagner & Debes, Leipzig

Nuremberg and Beyond
The Memoirs of Siegfried Ramler
From 20th Century Europe to Hawai'i

by Siegfried Ramler

Edited by Paul Berry

Designed by MacKinnon Simpson

Facing Page: I was born and raised in Vienna, Austria, then the cultural capital of Europe. My childhood home at 11 Lilienbrungasse is circled in Vienna's second district, Leopoldstadt.

DEDICATIONS

Siegfried Ramler: For David, Dita, Larry, and Malia,
Nā Keiki O ka ʻAina—Children of the Land—who toil for a better world …

Paul Berry: To historians and teachers of history, the keepers of the past …

MacKinnon Simpson: To my lifelong friend Joan Sugerman - writer, producer, director, and filmmaker extraordinaire!

PUBLISHER:
Ahuna Press
921 Maunawili Circle
Kailua, Hawaiʻi 96734

ISBN: 978-0-9706213-4-4

Hard cover trade edition
Printed in China
First trade edition, December 2008

School excursion to the Vienna woods with the classmates from the Vienna Sperlgymnasium, a secondary school. I am circled.

PREFACE

Siegfried Ramler's *Memoir* deserves wide readership, as it covers a career and events spanning eight decades on four continents, and remains relevant for all interested in international criminal justice. As a young man finding his way in an uncertain postwar world, Ramler contributed significantly to the processes that instituted international criminal law, including the concept of waging aggressive war and committing crimes against humanity. With Ramler as key interpreter during interrogations and in the courtroom, Nuremberg jurists and linguists established the standards and processes that made possible the present international criminal tribunals dealing with crimes in the former Yugoslavia, Rwanda, and elsewhere.

The attitudes and reactions of those on trial in Nuremberg remain instructive for today's criminal lawyers and students of international criminal law. As an interpreter Ramler had close contact with such famous Nazi leaders as Hermann Göring and Rudolph Hess, allowing readers to see these historic figures in close up during their interrogations and courtroom proceedings.

His description of the Nazi Anschluss of Austria, the ravages of Kristallnacht in Vienna, and his experiences through the nightly bombings of London make for captivating reading. That he was subsequently able to turn his talents and experiences into effective international education for so many young people offers testimony to the heart and energy that Ramler has brought to everything he has undertaken. As a war observer, family man, linguist, scholar, international educator, and simultaneous interpreter, Ramler has a life story that chronicles an era and provides excellent reading.

Siegfried Ramler is one those rare people who make all who know him feel fortunate in being touched by his indomitable spirit.

Justice Richard J. Goldstone,
Former Chief Prosecutor for the International Tribunals for Rwanda and the former Yugoslavia

A group of Viennese Hitler Youth saluting Baldur von Schirach, Hitler Youth Leader and Gauleiter of Vienna after the Anschluss in 1938, when Austria was taken over by Germany. To escape rising persecutions, the Ramler family left Vienna within the next year. After the war, von Schirach was tried at Nuremberg and found guilty of crimes against humanity. He spent twenty years at Spandau Prison.

vii

FOREWORD

Life journeys, by their nature, are unique. Siegfried Ramler's was most special. From his childhood in Vienna to the dangers of Nazi annexation, to escape to wartime London via Kindertransport, to his work as a linguist at the Nuremberg Trials, Siegfried Ramler's life was intertwined with historic events of the 20th century.

Then Hawai'i intervened. First in the form of a native daughter of the islands who worked as a court reporter at Nuremberg. That friendship deepened into love, and led to marriage in Paris. A career in Hawai'i followed, first in language instruction, and then in international education that focused on the Asia-Pacific region.

Like Hawai'i, Siegfried Ramler's life reflects multicultural diversity, outreach, and a healthy regard for mutual understanding and respect.

Daniel K. Inouye
United States Senator

Hitler Youth formations march through the old city of Nuremberg in 1937. INSET: The recruitment poster translates: "Youth serves the Führer. All ten year-olds into the Hitler Youth." As in the companion Bund Deutscher Mädchen (League of German Girls), uniformed children were indoctrinated in the Nazi movement at an early age with slogans, militaristic training and anti-Semitism.

A family passes an eatery with a stenciled sign in the window reading: "This business is led by the union of the professional organization of restaurateurs of the N.S.D.A.P. Jews not welcome." The NSDAP is short for *Nationalsozialistische Deutsche Arbeiterpartei* (in English: National Socialist German Workers' Party), or Nazi Party.

Portraits of the Author as a Young Man

Siegfried Ramler, Vienna, 1934, age 10

Siegfried Ramler, Vienna, 1935, age 11

Siegfried Ramler, Vienna, 1927, age 3

Siegfried Ramler, Vienna, 1936, age 12

CHAPTERS

1

VIENNA
1924-1938

Early in the 20th century, my parents emigrated to Austria from the Galicia region of Poland, now belonging to Ukraine. The youngest of three children, I was born and spent my childhood years in Vienna's second district, also called Leopoldstadt. The enclave was populated by a mix of Austrians, Czechs, Hungarians, and Poles, as well as a sizable Jewish population, all part of the influx into Vienna of residents of the former Austro-Hungarian Empire. Driven by persecutions and economic hardships in Poland, my family saw life in Vienna, the Austrian capital, as an opportunity for a better life.

Located adjacent to the Danube's tributary, Donaukanal, Leopoldstadt was just a short walk across bridges to Vienna's inner city, which housed Vienna's commercial, government, and entertainment centers. Leopoldstadt was primarily a residential neighborhood of families of modest means. We lived in a simply furnished third-floor

Leopoldstadt Coat of Arms

walkup along a cobble-stoned narrow street, lined with low-rise apartment houses. Our family's social center was the kitchen, where we ate most of our meals. The living room was reserved for occasions when guests would visit. Long before the advent of supermarkets, my mother would shop at small grocery stores, butchers, and bakers, where customers were well known to the shopkeepers and credit was extended. My mother frequently sent me to pick up provisions at a nearby grocery owned by a Hungarian family.

The secondary school that I attended from 1934 to 1938, the Sperlgymnasium, was within walking distance of our apartment. Several of my schoolmates lived along our street, and we would gather after school for pickup soccer games in a nearby park with teams of two to four players. Ball playing in the park was forbidden. One of our friends was posted as a lookout to give us a signal so we could run away when a gendarme approached. Other than spontaneous soccer games, I was not involved in athletics except as an avid fan of the Austrian football league, which I followed through radio and the newspaper.

My Vienna was far removed from the Vienna of operettas, waltzes, and *Kaffeehaus* society. My Vienna was a city of

One of the most important cultural shrines in Austria, Vienna's baroque Schönbrunn Palace and its surrounding gardens are listed by UNESCO as a World Heritage Site. The palace and its grounds were completed around 1770 during the reign of Maria Theresia and served as the cultural center of the Habsburg Empire. In 1762 six-year-old musical prodigy Wolfgang Amadeus Mozart made his royal debut for the Empress and her guests in the Palace's parlor. When the Habsburg Empire collapsed in 1918, following its defeat in World War I, the newly created Austrian Republic preserved the edifice as a museum. During World War II the palace was damaged by Allied bombing, but it was restored after the war. In 1961 it served as the summit meeting place for John F. Kennedy and Nikita Khrushchev.

Wien. K. k. Prater. — Riesenrad.

Wurstelprater Amusement Park is located within the Viennese park known as the Prater. The entire area was once an aristocratic hunting ground but almost two-and-a-half square miles of it was made a public park in 1766 by Emperor Joseph II. Small restaurants and cafes were soon followed by carousels. The Park's giant ferris wheel—the Riesenrad—is 209' high and was built in 1897. Destroyed by Allied bombs in 1945, it was rebuilt in 1946. Today the Riesenrad is still a popular attraction for Viennese and tourists.

sounds. I remember the haunting music of a street organ-grinder playing Strauss melodies which wafted up to the windows of our apartment. Along the street below pushcart vendors hawked their wares and offered to sharpen kitchen knives. My first experiences with Mozart came from hearing radios playing orchestral music in our building.

On Sundays my father would take me to the Prater, a large amusement park famous for its *Riesenrad*, the huge ferris wheel at the entrance of the park that featured prominently in the Orson Welles film *The Third Man*. We would stop at one of the cafés along the Prater's promenades for ice cream or for a slice of a Viennese torte. My father also took me to the palace of Schönbrunn in Vienna's outskirts, where Emperor Franz Josef had reigned and died. With its majestic setting, baroque architecture, and sumptuous decor, Schönbrunn made a big impression on me. It is now a UNESCO World Heritage site.

One of my uncles on my mother's side was in the textile business, and owned a summer cottage and a little orchard on the outskirts of Vienna where we would sometimes visit on weekends. My first experience of riding in a motor vehicle, taking a taxi to the cottage, felt like a luxurious adventure.

When I visited Vienna in the spring of 2005, I retraced my footsteps to the old apartment and also to my old school. I called on the school's director, a charming lady who greeted me warmly and produced my attendance records from 1934 to 1938.

Thinking back to my secondary education in Vienna, I have memories of several excellent teachers of German language and literature. In particular, I recall learning great poetry, such as the odes of Goethe and Schiller, and the requirement to learn and recite poems by heart. This experience contributed significantly to my affinity

My father Lazar and I in our Vienna apartment. I am wearing the traditional Lederhosen.

for languages and to the development of a *Sprachgefühl*, a feeling for language, which was to stand me in good stead in my later career as a language teacher. I would convey to my students that, beyond vocabulary and structure, the use of language becomes enriched through the application of tone and sound, and through a transmission of feeling and sensibility, expressed especially strongly in poetry. By reading aloud and memorizing poetry, I would internalize the rhythm and beauty of language.

An example of the popular Wild West adventures, Chief Winnetou and his Silberbüchse (The Silver Gun), that I read as a youth in Vienna.

I also earned good marks in Latin, a favorite subject. I recall an enthusiastic teacher who would not accept Latin's designation as a dead language, and who engaged our class in animated Latin conversation. No doubt my background in Latin facilitated my later studies of French language and literature. History was also especially enjoyable, especially when taught by teachers whose presentations made the past come alive. Unfortunately I had no such affinity for mathematics, which never came easily.

I have fond memories of school excursions to the woods and hills around the Vienna region, led by a popular teacher who devoted weekends to accompanying his students. In my early adolescence in Vienna, conversation with peers played an important role, particularly since I was an only son and my two sisters were several years older than I. For hours friends and I would walk and talk along Vienna's streets, exploring neighborhoods and parks. These conversations became a vehicle for sharing experiences and impressions, articulating opinions and developing self-confidence. In those days teachers lectured in front of the class, with little or no opportunity for classroom discussions. As a result, such conversations with peers fulfilled the need for self-expression.

My mother, Eugenia Ramler.

Starting at an early age, I was an avid reader, especially engrossed in the series of 19th century adventure novels written by German novelist Karl May. Many of the stories set in the American Wild West featured the heroic Apache chief Winnetou and his friend Old Shatterhand. Reading these popular novels, I was in good company; well-known Karl May fans included Albert Einstein and Herman Hesse. Another phase in my reading included Nordic mythological tales, so-called *Heldensagen*, including the Siegfried and Nibelungen saga, themes of Richard Wagner's operas. I'll never know whether these tales prompted my parents to choose Siegfried as my first name.

The exact nature of my father's business was never clear to me, except that his work involved textile commerce in cooperation with the uncle who occupied an apartment in our building. In that era children did not talk with

15685 T The Franzens-Ring, Vienna—Regarded by Many as Architecturally "the Finest Street in Europe."

A stereoscopic card picturing Franzensring in Vienna, "Regarded by Many as Architecturally 'the Finest Street in Europe." The edifice at left with the Greek portico is the Parliament House. The Gothic building with the splendid tower is Vienna's City Hall. These photos were taken with a special camera whose two lenses were slightly offset to provide a 3-dimensional effect when viewed in a Stereopticon, much like the later Viewmaster.

parents about their occupations. I remember my father as a quiet and gentle person, a calming influence on those around him. My mother, caring deeply for her family and actively following our educational progress, tended to be more temperamental. As self-motivated and obedient children, we gave our parents no problems, and I recall no incidents of teenage rebellion.

My sisters excelled in their studies, often studying with classmates for examinations. They also led active social lives with friends, going to parties and performances. I was too young to be included, but I took a vicarious interest. My younger sister, Lotte, later told me one of her teachers fell in love with her and even asked my parents for her hand. She did not take the proposal seriously and nothing came of it.

THE ANSCHLUSS

My memories of the Anschluss, the sudden annexation of Austria by Germany, bring up street scenes and sounds. I recall vividly the swastika banners hanging from Vienna's buildings, martial music blaring from radios, and storm troopers with swastika armbands marching in cadence along the streets. An ominous feeling foreshadowed danger in those days. My teachers were required to give the "Heil Hitler" salute at the beginning of class, followed by the students' choral response. For some of my teachers, this was repugnant, and they raised a limp arm without enthusiasm.

In 1934, several years before the Anschluss, Chancellor Engelbert Dollfuss, a conservative Austrian nationalist opposed to a union with Germany, was assassinated by Austrian Nazis. Unrest and increasing pressure from Germany followed. Dollfuss's successor, Kurt Schuschnigg, was summoned to Hitler's Berchtesgaden residence and forced to place Nazis in key positions of the Austrian cabinet. When Schuschnigg announced a plebiscite on the question of union with Germany, Hitler's response was the march into Austria, the total takeover of the government, and Schuschnigg's arrest and imprisonment.

The economic turbulence and hardships of the depression years in the 1930s created fertile ground for the Nazi movement in Austria, leaving Austria's political leadership vulnerable to German pressure. Facing no military opposition, the German Army Wehrmacht troops were welcomed by an enthusiastic and cheering population.

As for Austria's fate and role in the circumstances surrounding the Anschluss, two narratives were articulated: Austria as the first European victim nation in the path of Nazi aggression, and Austria as a willing and enthusiastic partner

While Austrian nationalists did not favor the 1938 annexation to Germany, most individual Austrians did. Enthusiastic Viennese girls welcome a German soldier after the Anschluss.

in joining the Reich. Both narratives resonate still as Austria contemplates its past.

With Nazi governance in Austria, anti-semitism, already a latent and growing phenomenon in Vienna, soon threatened the sizable Jewish population. Austrian Nazis rounded up Jews as they were leaving synagogues and made them clean city streets on their hands and knees while passersby jeered. Expropriation of Jewish businesses and property as well as dismissal from professions and government positions followed quickly. Jews, who had been prominent and influential in Austria's cultural and academic life, were purged from their positions, forced to emigrate, or sent to concentration camps. Sigmund Freud, who found refuge in England, was a famous emigrant, as were, among others, composer Arnold Schönberg and film director Billy Wilder.

An Austrian Nazi election poster honors Adolf Hitler, Austrian by birth. It reads: "Hitler Our Last Hope." and " Therefore Come to Us!"

Nazis humiliated Jews by forcing them to scrub Vienna's streets as crowds laughed. Anti-Semitism was rampant in Austria—of the 200,000 Jews living there in the 1930s, about half escaped and some 65,000 perished. Only about 10,000 Jews live in Austria now.

A cloth Star of David, symbol of Nazi persecution.

Streetcar adorned with swastikas and a sign advertising a speech by Reichsminister Rudolf Hess in support of the Anschluss. A referendum showed 99% of Austrian voters approved annexation.

Under a banner that reads: "We sing for Adolf Hitler," the Vienna Boys' Choir hails Hitler and his entourage during his first official visit to Vienna after the Anschluss.

Austro-Hungarian Theodor Herzl (1860-1904) founded political Zionism from his base in Vienna. It was a powerful movement—both my sisters joined—and, after the war, Zionism helped create the state of Israel.

Lotte Ramler

For my parents, social life centered around relatives, but also included a circle of close friends, called *Hausfreunde*, who would informally and without invitation drop in to see us and share lemon tea and cakes. When our family doctor made a house call to check on me when I had a cold or a fever, his visit tended to be more social than medical, chatting with my parents over tea.

During my childhood and early adolescence in Vienna, both my parents and older sisters doted on me, perhaps even spoiled me, as the only son and younger brother. The nickname given me by my sisters was *Bubi*, a diminutive of "Bube," the informal German designation for "boy." I can't help but think that the warmth and affection extended to me by my family had beneficial effects, giving me self-confidence that served me in my later life.

Adele Ramler

Inspired by its Viennese founder Theodor Herzl, my sisters participated in a strong Zionist movement in Vienna during the first decades of the 20th century. This movement rose in response to anti-Semitism and pogroms preceding the Nazi period, with manifestations in both Eastern and Western Europe.

For Theodor Herzl, the notorious and widely disseminated "Dreyfus Affair" became a cause célèbre which sparked his activism. Dreyfus was a French army artillery captain of Jewish faith, who had been falsely accused of treason. He was court-martialed, stripped of his military rank, and sent to Devil's Island. Eventually exonerated and fully reinstated, he fought in World War I. The highly publicized injustice of Dreyfus's conviction awakened in Herzl and his followers a Jewish feeling and need for emergence from the diaspora and a return to Zion through the establishment of a Jewish state.

In 1933, my older sister Adele, motivated by Zionist idealism, emigrated to Palestine, then under British rule, and joined a Kibbutz, an agricultural commune. To gain admission to Palestine, she had to obtain a coveted immigration certificate from British authorities. To allow two emigrants to be admitted with one certificate, Adele followed the practice of entering into a *pro-forma* marriage that was dissolved once she reached Palestine. A few years later, Lotte, my younger sister, joined Adele in Palestine. They both later married, raised families, and eventually settled in the seaport city of Haifa. With the annexation of Austria to Nazi Germany and its fatal consequences for Austrians of Jewish faith, my sisters' residence in Palestine, later to become Israel, turned into a life-saving refuge for our parents.

KRISTALLNACHT

My parents were anxious for me, their only son, to leave Austria and escape the Nazi regime. As for themselves, they received two weeks notice to vacate our apartment. With nowhere to go and an uncertain future, the urgent need for them to leave was heightened by a night of massive rampage throughout Germany and Austria against Jewish inhabitants, business establishments, and places of worship. This pogrom, the infamous "Kristallnacht," took place on the night of November 9, 1938, and was carried out under orders from Hitler in retaliation for the assassination in Paris of a German diplomat by a young Jewish Pole. Armed with incendiary materials and sledgehammers, SS and SA men, and Nazi storm troopers burned and smashed stores, synagogues, and shrines, and entered houses, beating and arresting Jewish inhabitants, herding them into a holding area and into trucks for transportation to camps. That night foreshadowed the Holocaust and the tragedies to follow.

Leopoldstadt, the second district, with its large Jewish population, was a particular target of Kristallnacht. I recall staying up and watching some of the destruction through the curtain of our apartment's window. When we saw SS men walking up our street, followed by trucks, my father went into hiding in our attic. With hearts pounding, we turned off the apartment's lights, hoping for danger to pass. To our relief the SS men did not enter the building and my father escaped arrest. However, my grandfather on my mother's side, living quietly with his wife in another area of Vienna, was arrested and taken to a concentration camp, where he perished. I remember my grandfather as kind and gentle, a gifted story-teller, whom we frequently visited in his Vienna apartment. His death, directly affecting my family, represents millions of Holocaust victims who were to follow.

I saw Kristallnacht as a particularly virulent expression of the Nazism which multiplied until Germany was defeated. At that time I had no way of knowing that later I would be directly involved in the process of bringing the perpetrators of this barbarism to justice.

Nazi Brownshirts nail up a sign on a Jewish business: "Not one penny to the Jews."

On the day following Kristallnacht the *Times* in London wrote the following editorial:

> "No foreign propaganda bent upon blackening Germany before the world could outdo the tale of burnings and beatings, of a blackguardly assault on defenseless and innocent people, which disgraced that country yesterday."

ESCAPE...THE KINDERTRANSPORT

In response to Kristallnacht and continuing dangers, the British Jewish Refugee Committee appealed to the British government to permit children under seventeen to enter Great Britain from Germany, Austria, and the Czech territories. This rescue operation, called "Kindertransport," was approved by Parliament after a debate in the House of Commons, and brought about 10.000 children to Britain, where they were received by foster families or hostels or on farms. Some eventually made their way to the United States or Canada. A number of the older ones joined the British armed forces as soon as they were eighteen and took part in the fight against the Nazis. I was lucky—most of them never saw their parents again.

The Kindertransport, which I joined in December of 1938, started within a month after Kristallnacht and ended when war broke out in September, 1939. For me, just fourteen years old at the time, England was a natural destination since two of my uncles were living in London and were ready to receive me there.

Recollections of the Kindertransport, the train ride from Vienna to Ostend, the adventure of crossing the foggy and stormy English Channel, and first impressions of London come back to me only as very vague vignettes. I do recall a strong feeling that this crossing meant a decisive break with the past and the beginning of an independent existence, free from parental constraints. At the time I had no feeling of abandonment, no anxieties about my future, but rather a sense of anticipation and excitement in facing a new life in England.

This sense of anticipation of an uncertain future, even welcoming the unknown, was to remain with me in my later life. Rather than looking back with homesickness or nostalgia, I eagerly looked forward to new opportunities and adventures. An affinity for English had already started through classes and readings, readying me for new encounters in England.

Kindertransport children were issued passports for their journey by Nazi officials. They traveled alone and were only permitted to take a few of their belongings along to life in a new land.

This statue, Children of the Kindertransport, was created by Frank Meisler, himself a child of the Kindertransport. It stands in the Liverpool Street Station in London, and a duplicate is scheduled to be installed in the main train station in Berlin.

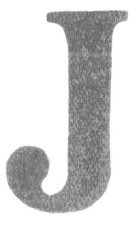

LEFT: Arriving safely in England, a Kindertransport teen seems to realize that she is alone, separated from her family, probably forever.

RIGHT: On the front page of the author's Kindertransport passport, a stamped red J stands for JUDE (jew).

OUR PARENTS ESCAPE . . . KLADOVO TRANSPORT

Having once fled from their place of birth in Galicia to a supposed haven in Austria, my parents for the second time in their lives faced the urgent need of escape from Vienna under Nazi rule. After the war broke out in 1939, many Viennese Jews, in danger of deportation to concentration camps in Poland, sought whatever ways they could to leave Austria.

On November 25, 1939 my parents joined a group of approximately 800 who left Vienna by rail for the Czech town of Bratislava, planning to sail to Palestine. There they were joined by hundreds of other refugees from Berlin and Danzig, and boarded several small vessels which were to take them down to the Danube delta for transfer to a larger ship for the journey to Palestine.

However, in one of the coldest winters of the century, the Danube froze, stranding the group in the Yugoslav harbor town of Kladovo.

During the winter months Kladovo became isolated and scarce provisions could only arrive by sled. Conditions aboard the overcrowded Danube barges were terrible. Lack of space and bunks required sleeping in shifts. Given the bad hygienic conditions, diseases were rampant, including scurvy and typhoid. After several months the Yugoslav authorities gave permission to the refugees to leave the barges. My parents, along with others, reached the Yugoslav town of Sabac where they awaited arrangements and papers to allow them to travel to Palestine and join their daughters.

At the very last moment, my older sister Adele, after months of efforts and calls on authorities, managed to obtain the certificates for our parents' entry to Palestine via rail, traveling through Bulgaria and Turkey. They were among a very small number of the original group which had left Austria the previous year. The very day after their departure from Sabac, Germany invaded Yugoslavia. Sabac was bombed, and the borders were closed. The remaining refugees who survived the bombing were rounded up and perished in concentration camps.

Miraculously my parents joined their daughters in Haifa at the end of 1940. They were to live out the remaining years of their lives there under the care of their family. I was able to see them in 1946 when I visited Palestine during a recess from my assignment in Nuremberg.

Three Yugoslavian riverboats, *Czar Dusan, Czar Nichola* and *Kraljica Marija,* which ferried Kladovo refugees along the Danube, docked for the winter at the port of Kladovo.

University of Hawai'i Map Collection (National Geographic map used with permission) Routes researched and created by Thorsten Büker and Boris Chomenko.

My Kindertransport trip between Vienna and London is traced in **BLUE**, and my parents' far longer escape from Vienna to Palestine is shown in **RED** on a 1938 map. Boat segments are indicated by dashed lines while train portions are solid. INSET: My family in Israel. Standing: My father Lazar and sisters Adele and Lotte. Seated: My mother Eugenia.

2

LONDON
1938-1944

In London a fundamental transition from dependence on my parents to considerable autonomy began for me. I stayed briefly at a youth hostel, then moved into my uncle's flat near Hampstead Heath. My uncle and aunt, also originally from Vienna, were retired and gave me considerable independence. Their only child, a daughter, had completed medical studies in Vienna and was a physician in New York, sharing a practice with her husband. After Pearl Harbor, when the United States entered the war, he joined the U.S. Army and became a medical officer serving in London and on the European continent, occasionally visiting us in the London apartment. My uncle and aunt were to join their daughter in New York in later years.

I combined work with studies, working first as an office boy in a furniture factory, and later, after the war broke out, operating a lathe in an armament factory. In the evenings I took courses at a London County Council school.

As I adapted from my native German to the use of English in daily life and in all my studies, language played a key role. At the armament factory I was surrounded by workers with a strong Cockney dialect, which was very strange to me at first but quickly became quite familiar. As I think of it now, the transition to English came to me naturally and rapidly, helped by making friends, both immigrants and British natives. At that time I also began to study French, an interest which intensified in my later career through residence and several study periods in France.

Soon after my arrival in England, Germany invaded Poland; the Second World War broke out and transformed my life in London. My uncle and aunt evacuated to the south of England, leaving me alone in their London apartment. Though they invited me to go with them, I insisted on staying in London to carry on with my work and studies. In the evenings, when not on night shift in the factory, I studied at one of the London County Council colleges taking basic courses.

Wartime London, with nightly German bombardment, known as the "Blitz," followed later by the unmanned buzz bomb drones, was marked by a unique spirit of sharing and friendliness among Londoners, quite different from the typical perception of British reserve and aloofness. Walking along the street after the air raid sirens had sounded, I would be invited by residents to join them in their shelter, or have drivers offer me a lift home. The platforms of the London

Firewatcher on the roof of a London building with St. Paul's Cathedral in background. I volunteered for the job as a firewatcher for my building in Stamford Hill , vulnerable to German bombs and rockets. The Blitz lasted seventy-six nights, targeting central London and the suburbs.

An oft-repeated scene of children returning home.

A V-2 rocket hit Battersea in January 1945 killing 22. Left: A canteen serves hot coffee to survivors. Right: A girl and her "Union Jack" among the ruins.

Newbury, Berkshire, England: Two bewildered ladies stand amidst the rubble of their almshouse home.

Undeterred by the building crumbling around them, Londoners browse the shelves of a library after bombs destroyed the roof.

underground stations, deep below the streets, filled up nightly with families who gathered for shelter in the company of friends and neighbors. Far from a besieged mood, the London tube took on the spirit of a block party with good humor, food, and music.

Most nights the sirens sounded as darkness fell, with the London sky lit up by searchlights and anti-aircraft fire, punctuated by the intermittent sound of explosions. One night, sleeping in my uncle's apartment, I was awakened by particularly heavy blasts. With a premonition of worse to come, I decided to go down to the basement where many of the building's occupants gathered for protection and slept on cots. Soon a bomb exploded across the street, violently shaking our building and causing plaster to fall from the basement's ceiling. When the all-clear signal sounded at dawn, I went up to the apartment and saw my bed totally covered with collapsed furniture, glass, and debris.

By going down to the cellar in time, I had escaped injury or possibly death.

Emerging from shelters after a night of air raids, I often saw evidence of bomb damage in the vicinity of my uncle's apartment with feelings of relief at having escaped but also with a heightened sense of vulnerability. The V-1 buzz bombs, delivered by unmanned drones, were particularly nerve-racking. I would hear the approaching noise of the drone overhead, followed by an eerie silence, the wait for the explosion, then the sirens of fire trucks and ambulances. I could never know where or when one of these drones would strike. Work at the factory, often on the night shift, provided

SHELTER FULL
except to reserved ticket holders
NEAREST PUBLIC SHELTER

SHELTERERS' BEDDING
The practice of shaking bedding over the platforms, tracks and in the subways is strictly forbidden

During the war, many London subway stations, popularly called Tube stations, were used as public air-raid shelters. Here a mother tucks her child in bed for the night, using bunks that have been built in a tunnel Some stations in populous areas became so crowded that they were reserved only for nearby residents who had made reservations (upper sign) and who had been issued tickets. This ticketing system guaranteed regular Tube shelterers their platform space and was a great improvement on the prior arrangement, in which large numbers of people queued daily outside the station. In less populous areas, like this small side service tunnel with no tracks, accommodations were far less cramped. These air-raid shelters gave people a safe gathering place and created a one-for-all atmosphere that contributed a war-winning attitude. Hitler's bet that his terror bombing campaign would force the British populace into demanding that their government sue for peace backfired.

modest income and brought me close to my co-workers. I treasure those London days when I lived through "Britain's finest hours," as expressed so memorably by Winston Churchill in his writings and broadcasts.

I recall gathering around the radio with neighbors in the apartment building, following news of the war's progress, and listening to the special cadence of Churchill's speeches. This sentence from one of the broadcasts still rings in my ears: "We shall defend our island whatever the cost may be; we shall fight on the beaches, landing grounds, in fields, in streets and on the hills. We shall never surrender."

With the presence of Allied soldiers at England's military bases, including Yanks volunteering prior to America's formal entry into the war, London took on an international look, which D-Day preparations and support for the Allied invasion of the continent later amplified. General de Gaulle, heading the Free French movement, established his headquarters in London, and contingents of European army units, including Polish and Dutch forces, joined the British and American troops in preparation for the invasion.

For a young man in his late teens and early twenties, life in wartime London had a special aura. British and Allied soldiers would come to London from their bases along the coast, frequenting pubs and dance halls. With a circle of male and female friends, some British and some immigrants, I developed an interest in music hall performances, went to Picadilly's large cinemas showing big production films, and frequented clubs in London's West End. My income from work at the factory, while modest, allowed me to afford some of these pleasures. Reshaped by the war, London gave me a heightened, somewhat feverish sense of the present, with a doubtful, undefined future.

My English skills developed rapidly through use in daily life, classes and individual reading. A favorite author at the time was P.G. Wodehouse. I became addicted to his *Jeeves* novels, enjoying his special quality of British humor. Writing effective English prose also became a challenge. Coming from a tradition of German writing where sentences with long adverbial clauses were usual and acceptable, I tried to transform my written English expression, aiming at a crisp and direct style with limited but well targeted use of vocabulary. Within a relatively short time, I achieved bilingual competence in German and English, followed later by mastery of French. These language skills equipped me for my duties at the Nuremberg trials and later for my career of teaching European languages and literature.

August 31, 1944: American crooner Bing Crosby, star of stage, screen and radio, sings to Allied troops at the London stage door canteen in Piccadilly.

National Archives & Records Administration

National Archives & Records Administration

The Siegfried Line was a series of massive ramparts and tank traps along the German-French border. As U.S. Army troops moved into German villages and cities, bilingual interpreters were needed to deal with surrendering German units and with billeting and provisions for U.S. forces. I responded to a call for linguists, passed a test, and was assigned as an aide to Allied troops crossing into Germany.

Library of Congress

British wartime Prime Minister Winston Churchill strikes a determined pose. At an early stage in the war Churchill advocated summary execution of leading Nazis. However, he was dissuaded from this position by U.S. pressure and supported the judicial proceedings at Nuremberg.

In London in November 1942, aged 18.

THE LONDON BLITZ

December 29, 1940: A vision emerges from the smoke. Despite being targeted by the German bombers, and absorbing several minor hits, St. Paul's Cathedral survived the Blitz.

An ambulance crew searches a collapsed building for victims.

For some eight months, from September 7, 1940 to May 10, 1941, the London Blitz was a relentless, nightly experience, with air raid sirens sounding at dusk and the all-clear signal at dawn. At that time I lived alone in my uncle's apartment in the Stamford Hill district. My relatives had evacuated to Surrey, to the south of England, but I preferred to stay in London, carrying on with studies and war work in a factory. Several of my friends had also come to England as refugees and, like me, lived alone, working or studying under similar circumstances. We formed close friendships, getting together in the evenings, playing cards and talking. Living through dangerous times forges close bonds, as certainly was true of Londoners during the Blitz.

When existentialist philosopher Jean Paul Sartre wrote about authentic feeling and authentic behavior, he made the point that in times of extreme danger, such as in wartime under bombardment or in a front line foxhole, man achieves the highest potential of authenticity, of expressing genuine feelings. I ask myself now if I experienced fear at that time. Certainly I was aware of the carnage around me, coming across bombed out buildings which I had entered a day before, and hearing the sirens of ambulances taking the wounded to hospitals. Rather than fear, however, I felt a heightened sense of awareness, of living through a highly charged time.

Returning to my apartment in the evening after work, I drew the blinds—a black-out was strictly enforced—and ate my supper, often fish and chips, a London staple wrapped in newspaper which I had picked up from a stand on the way home. Soon after the siren sounded, searchlights would sweep across the rooftops and the ack-ack of anti-aircraft batteries would start up, at times from a distance and at times nearby and very loud, punctuated intermittently by exploding bombs. Once or twice a week I had firewatch duty for our building. Wearing a helmet and equipped with a bucket of sand and a fire extinguisher, I would spend several hours on the building's roof, looking out for incendiary danger.

Among the correspondents filing dispatches from London during the Blitz was the American Ernie Pyle, later awarded a Pulitzer prize. He captures vividly the feeling of a London night raid in the winter of 1940:

It was a night when London was ringed and stabbed with fire. They came just after dark, and somehow you could sense from the quick, bitter firing of the guns that there was to be no monkey business this night.

Shortly after the sirens wailed you could hear the Germans grinding overhead. In my room, with its black curtains drawn across the windows, you could feel the shake from the guns. You could hear the boom, crump, crump, crump, of heavy bombs at their work of tearing buildings apart. They were not too far away.

Half an hour after the firing started I gathered a couple of friends and went to a high, darkened balcony that gave us a view of a third of the entire circle of London. As we stepped out onto the balcony a vast inner excitement came over all of us—an excitement that had neither fear nor horror in it, because it was too full of awe.

You have all seen big fires, but I doubt if you have ever seen the whole horizon of a city lined with great fires—scores of them, perhaps hundreds.

There was something inspiring just in the awful savagery of it. The closest fires were near enough for us to hear the crackling flames and the yells of firemen. Little fires grew into big ones even as we watched. Big ones died down under the firemen's valor, only to break out again later.

About every two minutes a new wave of planes would be over. The motors seemed to grind rather than roar, and to have an angry pulsation, like a bee buzzing in blind fury.

The guns did not make a constant overwhelming din as in those terrible days of September. They were intermittent—sometimes a few seconds apart, sometimes a minute or more. Their sound was sharp, near by; and soft and muffled, far away. They were everywhere over London.

Into the dark shadowed spaces below us, while we watched, whole batches of incendiary bombs fell. We saw two dozen go off in two seconds. They flashed terrifically, then quickly simmered down to pin points of dazzling white, burning ferociously. These white pin points would go out one by one, as the unseen heroes of the moment smothered them with sand. But also, while we watched, other pin points would burn on, and soon a yellow flame would leap up from the white center. They had done their work—another building was on fire.

The greatest of all the fires was directly in front of us. Flames seemed to whip hundreds of feet into the air. Pinkish-white smoke ballooned upward in a great cloud, and out of this cloud there gradually took shape—so faintly at first that we weren't sure we saw correctly—the gigantic dome of St. Paul's Cathedral.

St. Paul's was surrounded by fire, but it came through. It stood there in its enormous proportions—growing slowly clearer and clearer, the way objects take shape at dawn. It was like a picture of some miraculous figure that appears before peace-hungry soldiers on a battlefield.

The streets below us were semi-illuminated from the glow. Immediately above the fires the sky was red and angry, and overhead, making a ceiling in the vast heavens, there was a cloud of smoke all in pink. Up in that pink shrouding there were tiny, brilliant specks of flashing light-antiaircraft shells bursting. After the flash you could hear the sound.

Up there, too, the barrage balloons were standing out as clearly as if it were daytime, but now they were pink instead of silver. And now and then through a hole in that pink shroud there twinkled incongruously a permanent, genuine star—the old-fashioned kind that has always been there.

Below us the Thames grew lighter, and all around below were the shadows—the dark shadows of buildings and bridges that formed the base of this dreadful masterpiece.

Later on I borrowed a tin hat and went out among the fires. That was exciting too; but the thing I shall always remember above all the other things in my life is the monstrous loveliness of that one single view of London on a holiday night—London stabbed with great fires, shaken by explosions, its dark regions along the Thames sparkling with the pin points of white-hot bombs, all of it roofed over with a ceiling of pink that held bursting shells, balloons, flares and the grind of vicious engines. And in yourself the excitement and anticipation and wonder in your soul that this could be happening at all.

These things all went together to make the most hateful, most beautiful single scene I have ever known.

Ernie Pyle

The bombing of London marked a shift in German strategy from destroying military and strategic targets, such as bases and airfields, to having a psychological impact on the British populace. Hitler was convinced that England would fold under the relentless pressure of nightly bombing of cities and landmarks. Londoners bonded and rallied with renewed determination to resist Nazi aggression, proving him fatally wrong. Allied forces made England a staging ground in preparation for D-Day, when the tide of the war would turn toward the sure defeat of Germany.

SUDDENLY . . . GUIDED MISSILES

The Blitz of London ended in early May 1941, when Hitler shifted his Luftwaffe east for the Russian offensive. While England would never again suffer the sustained raids of the Blitz, two frightening new weapons— the V-1 flying bomb and V-2 rocket—were pointed at London. The "V" in the missiles' name stood for "Vergeltungswaffen" which translates to "Retaliation/Vengeance Weapon."

German rocket scientist Werner Von Braun, who later guided the United States space venture to the moon, headed up the Nazi's secret rocket program at Peenemünde on the Baltic Sea in northern Germany.

The V-1 was the first guided missile ever used in war. Jet-powered, it was launched from a modified plane or catapulted off a tilted rack aimed, approximately, at its target. By the standards of today's GPS-guided cruise missiles, it was crude, crashing to earth once its fuel was exhausted. It caused great terror with its loud buzzing sound—hence the nickname "buzz bomb"—then went completely silent just before hitting. The V-2 was an actual rocket and much more sophisticated.

Von Braun, who had already been jailed by the Gestapo for defeatist thinking (and released under orders from a very high level), was interested in rockets for space travel, not as weapons, and upon hearing the news that the first V-2 had hit London, exclaimed, "The rocket worked perfectly except for landing on the wrong planet." He later described it as his "darkest day."

Using concentration camp labor, the Nazis built about 30,000 V-1 missiles. Some 10,000 were fired at England between June 13, 1944 and March 29, 1945. The rest were never launched, destroyed in bombing raids, or fired at the Low Countries, especially Antwerp, Belgium, where men and

One of Hitler's V-1 rockets plunging to earth in London. It will explode on impact.

V-1 cutaway.

National Archives and Records Administration

supplies were pouring in to reinforce the Allied armies then slogging across Europe. 2,419 V-1s actually reached London, killing 6,184 people and injuring some 17,981.

The V-1's altitude and speed posed different problems than attacking bombers had during the Blitz. V-1s were small and fast-moving, and hard to bring down with the anti-aircraft guns of the day. With no pilot, oxygen system, and complex engine, the V-1 didn't have many vulnerable points, and they flew faster than most fighters. Some 2,000 barrage balloons were deployed, but the Germans countered with cable cutters on the V-1's wings leading edges, and less than 300 V-1s were actually destroyed by the balloons' tethering cables.

The biggest defensive breakthrough were electronic aids for the anti-aircraft guns, created at MIT's Radiation Lab in Cambridge, Massachusetts. These were radar-based and equipped with a proximity fuse. Once these improvements were installed, the rate of V-1s which got through diminished.

From a military standpoint, the Nazi regime designed the V-1 and V-2 flying bomb and rocket programs to reverse Allied advances on the European continent, hoping these powerful weapons would snatch victory from defeat. These innovative weapons did inflict terror, but sophisticated anti-aircraft guns and fighter planes diminished their impact as the war came to an end.

NUREMBERG
1945-1949

After D-Day in 1944, as the tide of the European front turned in favor of the Allies with their advance across the continent into Germany, the need arose for German-speaking linguists to help with the disarmament of the German forces and with logistics for the Allied occupation of Germany. When a call went out for linguists, I took a test in London, was accepted quickly, and was assigned to the U.S. 9th Air Force Service Command, which had the task of disarming segments of the Luftwaffe, the German Air Force. Issued an American uniform as special civilian staff, I was flown to an air base in France aboard a C-47, the work horse of the U.S. Air Force. Twenty-one years old, wearing a smart Eisenhower jacket and khaki trousers, I eagerly looked forward to this assignment.

Seated in the airplane's spartan bucket seat, I had my first experience of flying. Once in France, I spent several days riding in a Jeep making contact with the rearguard of Allied troops advancing into Germany at war's end and searching for the battalion I was supposed to join. I recall a chaotic and confusing journey, witnessing German towns and villages in a state of collapse, with refugees and stray soldiers clogging the roads, until the driver finally caught up with the unit I was to join.

I handled logistics in support of the mobile battalion, requisitioning housing and materials for the troops and officers as we moved from town to town. Several of the battalion's officers and I would drive in Jeeps ahead of the men, trucks, and armored vehicles until we reached the town designated as our next base. We would quickly locate a large school or public building suitable for lodging our men and order its immediate clearance prior to the battalion's arrival. For the officers, we would locate a residential part of the town and requisition several houses, typically to accommodate two officers per house. Serving as interpreter, I would give the house's occupants one hour to clear the premises, allowing them to take along only items they could carry. In most cases the families would move in with neighbors or relatives. After our officers had occupied the requisitioned houses, the owners would often return and ask for items, such as bedding or kitchen utensils, to be released to them. With few exceptions the American officers went along with such requests. These requisitions were carried out as temporary measures and houses would be returned to their owners or rightful occupants after the battalion had moved on. While it was unpleasant to evict people from their homes, I approached

Nuremberg's gigantic Zeppelin Field parade ground, site of the annual Nazi Party Congress. Hitler addressed cheering masses from the huge podium. Nuremberg's symbolic role as a cradle of Nazism played a key part in choosing the city for the International War Crimes Tribunal. L-R: S.S. Chief Heinrich Himmler, Adolf Hitler and S.A. Chief Viktor Lutze walk up to the World War I cenotaph to lay a wreath.

NAZI CEREMONIES AT NUREMBERG

National Archives & Records Administration

The Nazi propagandists staged massive ceremonies swirling with swastikas and featuring Wagnerian martial music. The Zeppelin Field complex in Nuremberg was designed by Hitler's favorite architect, Albert Speer. This September 1937 Nazi rally featured Speer's *Cathedral of Light;* 134 flak searchlights cast their beams thousands of feet into the night sky all around Zeppelin Field, to symbolize the four walls of a building.

Heinrich Himmler and Adolf Hitler review an elite SS unit during a Nuremberg ceremony. Himmler headed the Schutzstaffel (SS) and the Gestapo secret police. He was in direct charge of the Nazis' extermination camps and the *Einsatzgruppen* (task forces) often described as death squads. These were para-military units assigned to kill Jews and Nazi opponents.

Mesmerized Germans perform a synchronized *Hitlergruss* (Hitler salute) at the 1937 Reichsparteitag celebrations in Nuremberg.

SA troops parade past Adolf Hitler during the 1935 Reichsparteitag (the Third Reich party convention) in Nuremberg. Called the Blutfahne (Blood Flag), the swastika flag behind Hitler was one of the Nazis' more revered objects. It had been carried during the failed 1923 Beer Hall Putsch when three Nazis were shot and killed by Munich police during the uprising. The flag was soaked in blood.

this task as politely as possible. Instances of Allied personnel "liberating" items from homes as souvenirs were quite common, especially in the early stages of the occupation, until strict standards were imposed. One of my duties as interpreter for the battalion required me to obtain various supplies from the town, such as bakery or other food items, though for the most part the battalion was self-sufficient.

As part of our disarmament duties, we gathered documents and files from German military bases and government buildings. I helped identify the information for transmission by courier to the Allied headquarters, where it would be evaluated for potential intelligence. In most cases these were routine documents, such as inventories and expense accounts, though collections by advancing troops from other areas would yield important research data relating to German armaments, such as rocket development.

When asked whether I would volunteer to teach conversational German to interested GIs and officers in the battalion, I gladly accepted. For most students, their interest focused on learning phrases to help them meet German girls. After they had learned to say in German such phrases as "May I walk with you?" or "You are very pretty," attendance dropped rapidly. Only a few serious students continued to study with me.

A non-fraternization order, which was largely ignored by GIs, prevailed during the early days of the occupation. My very first foreign language teaching experience occurred under these unusual postwar circumstances. Little did I know then that these informal foreign language lessons were the beginnings of a major career!

I thoroughly enjoyed my first contact with Americans, especially their spirit, humor, and can-do approach to challenges.

Library of Congress

Leni Riefenstahl, noted Nazi documentary filmmaker, was asked by Hitler to depict the 1934 party rally in Nuremberg. Despite its heavy propaganda message, the resulting film, *Triumph of the Will,* was famed for its technical innovations.

THE NUREMBERG SETTING

Before assignment to permanent quarters at a house in Nuremberg's residential suburbs, I was assigned an initial billet at the Grand Hotel, close to the old city. Nuremberg had been the target of heavy Allied bombing, reducing the old city to rubble. A wing of the hotel still bore damage from bombing, requiring me to walk across wooden planks to reach my room. However, the hotel's lobby, dining room, and bars functioned in good condition and formed the center of an animated social life. The international staff members gathered there at the end of their working day.

Occupying Nuremberg at the end of the war in the spring of 1945, American troops enthusiastically wave U.S. flags atop the massive pillars of Zeppelin Field, site of Nazi rallies. INSET: Soon after capturing Nuremberg, American soldiers dynamited the enormous metal swastika adorning Zeppelin Field. Adolf Hitler's "Thousand Year Reich" had lasted barely twelve years.

By the end of the war, Hermann Göring's Luftwaffe had been swept from the skies by relentless Allied air attacks. The ancient city of Nuremberg had many industrial targets—factories producing motorcyles, airplane engines, and ball bearings—and in the process of leveling them, much of the city was turned into rubble. Some 2,000 buildings dating to medieval times were damaged or destroyed, and both the Grand Hotel and the Palace of Justice suffered bomb damage, though were still operational. Here an American B-17 bomber (the "Flying Fortress") casts an ominous shadow over Nuremberg as it takes aerial photos of the city on a reconnaissance mission.

National Archives & Records Administration

The Palace of Justice, a large building complex located about a mile from the Grand Hotel, housed the main courtroom where the international trial took place and several smaller courtrooms for the subsequent proceedings. In addition, it provided offices and work areas for the international staff, including judges, prosecution and defense counsel, secretariat, court reporters, press, and the language staff to which I was assigned. In preparation for the trials, the building required modifications essential for courtroom functions, with appropriate spaces for judges, witnesses, audience gallery, and wiring for amplification and translation.

Adjacent to the main building was a detention structure with cells housing the 21 defendants and some witnesses, who were led by guards from their cells to interrogation rooms and later to the courtroom's dock when the trial was in session.

At war's end Germany was divided into four occupation zones representing France, Great Britain, the United States and the USSR. Because Nuremberg was in the American zone, the United States carried responsibility for trial logistics, administration, and security, including military police and guard duties.

Sheathed in scaffolding used to repair bomb damage, Nuremberg's Grand Hotel served as the billet and social headquarters for Allied staff at the Tribunal.

Collection of Sabine Eiche

A tranquil scene of Nuremberg before the war, titled "Pegnitzpartie at the Fischersteg." This postcard was one of a scenic set purchased at the 1933 Reichsparteitag (Nazi Party convention) held in Nuremberg.

The east wing of the Nuremberg Palace of Justice. Courtroom 600—where the proceedings were held—is behind the blanked out windows. Nuremberg was in the American zone, so U.S. military police units had responsibility for the security inside and out. This photo was taken on September 30, 1946, the day before the verdicts were passed down, and so security was especially tight.

PREPARATIONS FOR THE TRIALS

The captured principal leaders of Germany, both military and civilian, had been brought to Nuremberg from the places where they had been arrested. The city of Nuremberg was chosen for the conduct of the trials, partly because of the availability of a large court house and other suitable facilities, and partly for symbolic reasons: to try Nazi leaders at the site of the annual Nazi Party rallies.

While several leaders, notably Adolf Hitler, were dead or missing, the twenty-one defendants represented Nazi Germany's leadership from key sectors of the government. Such leaders as Hermann Göring, Rudolf Hess, and Joachim von Ribbentrop were among the defendants.

In August 1945, soon after the end of the war in the European theater, the London Charter, with representation in its framing by the four prosecuting nations—United States,

Great Britain, France, and the Soviet Union—set the basis and procedural framework for the Nuremberg trials. Given leave by President Truman from his service as an associate justice of the U.S. Supreme Court to serve as U.S. Chief Prosecutor, Justice Robert H. Jackson played a leading role in the difficult task of building a consensus for the conduct of the trial. The United States and Great Britain approached the task from their tradition of Anglo-Saxon common law, France from the background of continental civil law, and the Soviet Union with a preference for summary justice and impatience with legal procedures. Rejecting summary justice, Jackson in his opening statement as U.S. Chief Prosecutor made this powerful statement:

> "We must never forget that the record on which we judge these defendants is the record on which history will judge us tomorrow. To pass these defendants a poisoned chalice is to put it to our lips as well. We must summon such detachment and intellectual integrity to our task that this trial will commend itself to posterity as fulfilling humanity's aspirations to do justice."

Despite disagreements and tensions, with a near breakdown of negotiations in London on questions of procedures and selection of defendants, it is to Jackson's credit that an agreement was achieved in a relatively short time, and that the international tribunal could be convened in Nuremberg. The resulting charter provided for a trial presided over by a four-power international tribunal, which was to render judgment and impose sentences.

The selection of the twenty-one defendants posed a challenge and required agreement and compromise by the four prosecuting nations. Two criteria played a role in the selection. Some defendants represented the leadership of the main sectors of the Nazi government—military, diplomatic, police and security, economy, and propaganda. Other defendants were selected and indicted because there was evidence regarding their roles and involvement in the leadership and decision-making linked to crimes.

Supreme Court Associate Justice Robert H. Jackson was selected by President Truman as the U.S. Chief Prosecutor and was instrumental in setting the trials in Nuremberg.

Several defendants were charged on each of the four counts of the indictment: crimes against peace, conspiracy to wage aggressive war, war crimes, and crimes against humanity. Others were charged on only one, two, or three specific counts, such as war crimes and crimes against humanity.

Because it was the first time in history that such charges were tried before an international court, Nuremberg broke new ground and established a milestone in the practice and implementation of international law. These trials set the precedent for the Tokyo trials that followed a year later. The precedent has carried over to the trials involving the former Yugoslav leaders, to the trials involving the genocide in Rwanda, and to indictments before the current International Criminal Court. Nuremberg also established the principle that following superior orders cannot excuse the commission of the crimes charged under the indictment.

JOINING THE NUREMBERG TRIBUNAL

About a month after the war's end in the European theater, my battalion reached the town of Erlangen in Franconia, located close to the city of Nuremberg. Having heard that a trial of German leaders was about to take place in that city's Palace of Justice, I took a Jeep, drove to Nuremberg, and called on the Adjutant-General's office for information pertaining to the trials. When the staff officer heard about my background and my current assignment to an air force battalion, he told me of the urgent need in Nuremberg for linguists in preparation for the trials, and expressed strong interest in my joining the staff. He said that the Office of U.S. Chief of Counsel, the administrative unit preparing for the trial, would take care of the details for my transfer, arrange for billets, and assign me to the language team working on document translation and pretrial interrogations.

However, when I approached the colonel in charge of my battalion, a gruff regular army officer, he refused to let me transfer and insisted that I would have to return to England when my duties were terminated. He was totally uninterested in the trials being prepared in Nuremberg, where he had no jurisdiction. Indeed, a short time later I received orders to report to an air base near Frankfurt for a flight back to England. After my driver dropped me off at the air base in the afternoon for a flight early the following morning, I faced a dilemma. Given the chaotic conditions in Germany at war's end and separate chains of command, I realized that it would be all but impossible to return to Nuremberg from London. I would have had no contact or standing to obtain a placement in Nuremberg, which was in the American zone of occupation.

I spent a restless night agonizing over a decision. Should I follow the order and board the aircraft for London the next

Charged with kidnapping, enslavement, extermination, and crimes against humanity, former Obergruppenführer and SS General Warner Lorenz is questioned by interpreter Siegfried Ramler during the pretrial phase of the Nuremberg proceedings.

morning with very little chance of returning, or should I ignore the order and make my way to Nuremberg? At the age of 21, I had reached a turning point in my life. Instead of boarding the aircraft, I hitchhiked to Nuremberg, where I was welcomed without any questions, given a U.S. civil service rating, allocated a billet in Nuremberg's Grand Hotel, and assigned to the recently-established language division.

Though literally AWOL from my battalion, I had confidence that my status would be cleared, given the trial's importance and priority. Indeed, several weeks later U.S. military police tracked me down at the Nuremberg Palace of Justice, where the Adjutant General's office confirmed my position and cleared my status as a member of the Nuremberg staff. I often think back to that fork in my life's course and the implications of my decision to join the staff of the 20th century's major trial. That decision, ignoring an order, set the course of my personal and professional life.

Former Reichsmarschall Hermann Göring, now a common prisoner, reading in his cell. The flimsy table next to his bed was designed specifically to eliminate suicide by hanging, as it would not support a man's weight. Göring, however, would cheat the hangman by swallowing a cyanide pill shortly before his scheduled execution.

PRETRIAL INTERROGATIONS

Immediately after my arrival in Nuremberg, I was assigned to interrogations, starting early in the morning and often lasting late into the evening. These were designed to build the prosecution's case and validate documentary evidence. The interrogations involved defendants and witnesses called to clarify and explain a given segment of the prosecution's case.

The majority of the pretrial interrogations were conducted with defendants, with relatively few witnesses called by the prosecution for interrogation and for testimony at the trial.

Rather than relying on large numbers of witnesses, involving the logistics of bringing them to Nuremberg for the length of the trial, the prosecution relied greatly on the submission of documentary evidence supporting the indictment, such as strategic plans leading to aggressive war or decrees and orders leading to war crimes and crimes against humanity.

Guards brought the defendants up from their prison cells to one of the interrogation rooms in the Palace of Justice. Present in the room would be a prosecution lawyer, a court reporter, and the German-English interpreter, which was my function during the pretrial phase. The military defendants, such as Generals Keitel and Jodl, were dressed in uniforms without insignia. When they entered the room, they stood at attention, clicked their heels, and took a seat when asked to do so. Civilian defendants were dressed in suits. The lawyers assigned to conduct the pretrial interrogations, and later the preparation and conduct of the trials, were recruited from the United States, some in a civilian capacity and some as military officers, serving under auspices of the U.S. Chief of Counsel.

When I think back to my most memorable experiences during the four years I spent in Nuremberg—over a year with the international trial and three additional years with the subsequent proceedings—the interrogations in preparation for the major trial stand out, as Germany's erstwhile leaders presented spontaneous and unfiltered testimony. This was the first time, just weeks after their capture following the defeat and dissolution of Nazi Germany that these men were required to answer questions and comment on their roles during the regime. The interrogations often paralleled an autopsy, where doctors trace the development of a disease leading to the patient's death. Their testimony yielded "history in the raw," expressed spontaneously before formal testimony on the witness stand could be shaped and filtered by defense strategy.

Although the conduct of the first trial was international, with judges and prosecution representing the United States, Great Britain, France, and the Soviet Union, the bulk of pretrial interrogations was conducted by U.S. counsel. The transcript of the defendants' testimony was shared with British, French, and Soviet delegations, as well as with defense counsel.

Defendants were generally cooperative, even eager to express themselves and place their roles in a favorable light. Typically they would explain the context for a given act or decision, or place their own role into the chain of responsibility and command. The interrogations highlighted the Nazi regime's *Führerprinzip*, leadership principle, where ultimate authority was exercised by the leader, Adolf Hitler, whether in his capacity as commander-in-chief of the armed forces, as head of state, or as party leader. Having committed suicide in a Berlin bunker at war's end, Hitler remained a presence at the trial, emerging strongly through the testimony of the key members of government and his personal entourage.

During the pretrial phase the language interpretation required me to translate the counsel's questions into German, and the defendant's or witness's responses into English. Some of the accused, such as Göring and Ribbentrop, understood English but preferred to wait for the translation and respond in German, giving them time for reflection.

PATTERNS OF DEFENSE

Both the pretrial interrogations and trial testimony by defendants followed a consistent pattern. The Nuremberg tribunal rejected the defense invoking the *Führerprinzip*—the leadership principle—requiring obedience to superior orders without questioning their legality. It rejected the claim as an excuse for the commission of crimes, and as a consequence created a significant contribution to international law.

A second line of defense claimed that conditions in times of war and Germany's struggle for survival required extreme measures that would not have been taken in peace time. This defense claim was advanced against charges of war crimes and violations of the Geneva Convention.

> **Their [pretrial] testimony yielded "history in the raw," expressed spontaneously before formal testimony on the witness stand could be shaped and filtered by defense strategy.**

Confronted with the evidence of mass killings and gassings, all of the defendants adopted a third defense position, claiming ignorance and absence of responsibility. They shifted the burden of guilt to leaders who were no longer alive, such as the Führer himself, and to leading individuals such as SS Chief Heinrich Himmler, Gestapo Chief Reinhard Heydrich, and party leader Martin Bormann.

On several occasions the defense raised the *tu quoque* or "you also" retort, stating that Allied nations had committed similar or identical crimes with which the Nuremberg defendants were charged. These defense claims referred particularly to the alleged commission of war crimes by the Soviet Union. Upholding the prosecution's objection to such claims, the tribunal stated that the issues before the tribunal were limited to the indictment of the defendants, and that claims of crimes committed by other nations were not admissable.

LEGAL COUNSEL AT NUREMBERG

Defendants were able to select defense counsel of their choice and were given assistance by the secretariat in contacting and interviewing prospective counsel, and in establishing residence for counsel in Nuremberg. In profile, the German defense counsel seated in front of the dock revealed a seasoned and conservative group, mostly older than the defendants, reflecting experience, confidence, and gravitas. Many of the German lawyers understood English, monitored our interpretation, and occasionally would object if they thought a given translation was in error.

In contrast, the American counsel tended to be younger and less experienced. Even Justice Jackson lacked historical perspective in placing the Nuremberg trials into the context of political developments leading to Nazi power and aggression, as evidenced by problems he faced while cross-examining Göring. However, the Americans were fast learners, and what they lacked in experience they made up for in prosecutorial commitment and zeal. Justice Jackson was a superb writer and orator. His opening and closing statements rank among the most eloquent judicial presentations of the 20th century. Consider this impressive paragraph in his opening statement:

> "The wrongs which we seek to condemn and punish have been so calculated, so malignant, and so devastating that civilization cannot tolerate their being ignored, because it cannot survive their being repeated. That four great powers stay the hand of vengeance and voluntarily submit their captives to the judgment of the law is one of the most significant tributes that power has ever paid to reason."

With former Nuremberg prosecutors Telford Taylor and Drexel Sprecher at a Nuremberg staff reunion in Washington, DC.

British and French prosecution teams were understandably better equipped than Americans in dealing with the sequence of events leading to the trials. Leading British prosecutors, Sir Hartley Shawcross and Sir David Maxwell Fyfe, were quite impressive in their presentations and cross-examination skills. When Justice Jackson faltered in his cross-exam of Göring, allowing Göring to dominate the exchange, Fyfe was able to regain the momentum. The Russians, mostly in military uniform, were impatient with formality and tended to bore in on documentary evidence relating to specific crimes.

Presiding judge, Lord Justice Lawrence, was masterful in his management of the trial, alternating firmness with humor and British understatement. The interpreters at the microphone appreciated his understanding of the challenges we faced and his admonition to counsel and witnesses to speak slowly.

Abundant analysis of the Nuremberg Trials exists in many languages, written by participants, observers, and scholars regarding the evidence and the legal impact of this historical and legal milestone. In the decades since the trials, I have written about, spoken widely, and participated in panels, both in the United States and abroad, dealing with various facets of the trial's legacy and impact.

THE CHALLENGES OF
SIMULTANEOUS INTERPRETATION

As preparations for trial began, a major linguistic hurdle had to be overcome. How could we make trial proceedings and documents understandable to judges, prosecutors, defendants, and defense counsel in Courtroom 600, as well as to audiences around the world following the proceedings?

Previous international gatherings had focused primarily on diplomatic issues and assumed that principals would speak and understand at least French or English.

At Nuremberg, however, interpretation and document translation were required into four languages: English, German, Russian, and French. Consecutive interpretation, translating in turn each statement, question, and response into each of the four languages, was not an acceptable option, since it would have been intolerably long and cumbersome. Furthermore, neither the prosecution staff, nor German defense counsel, nor the tribunal could be expected to deal with the complex legal and historical issues in a language other than their own. The Nuremberg trials were the first media event after World War II. Print and broadcast journalists required instant accounts. These challenges were the impetus to create a system of simultaneous interpretation, now in general use throughout the world, but pioneered on a large scale by our group at Nuremberg.

We had no body of experience to draw on, and had to develop the necessary skills on our own. It required interpreters who were linguistically and mentally able to rise to that challenge, as well as installation of equipment necessary for the transmission of language channels through earphones.

We created teams of twelve interpreters, with three persons on each of the four language microphones located in booths divided by glass panels. Thus the Russian booth would have three individuals: one translating German into Russian, and the other two, English and French into Russian, respectively. The eight members of the tribunal, the prosecution and defense staffs, the defendants, and the courtroom audience wore earphones and had a selector switch to tune in to any of the four languages. The original

Hermann Göring was overheard to say: "This system is very efficient, but it will also shorten my life!"

language on the courtroom floor would come through verbatim on a given channel. This technology, primitive by today's standards, was supplied by IBM. After the trials started, Hermann Göring was overheard to say: "This system is very efficient, but it will also shorten my life!"

We realized that the interpreter's personality and tone of voice must not detract from the testimony. The aim, ideally, was for the listener to accept the voice coming through the earphones as that of the original speaker. Nevertheless, there were interesting variations in the way some early interpreters performed. One rather laconic fellow gave the shortest possible rendition of long sentences, leaving the audience wondering what they were missing.

Occasionally an interpreter would freeze, either because of a translation difficulty or because of a shock effect arising from the nature of the testimony. A monitor would flash a light, halting the proceedings and allowing the interpreter to regain composure. As with traffic, we developed a system of orange and red lights which would be flashed by the monitor, signaling speakers in the courtroom. The yellow light was a signal to slow down and to prevent two parties from speaking

The site of the Nuremberg International Military Tribunal, Courtroom 600 in the Palace of Justice had been re-configured for these trials. The interpreters' booth is at upper left. I am on the German-to-English microphone third from left behind the glass. (red circle)

at the same time. The red light, used sparingly, gave a sign to the presiding judge to declare a short recess.

During recruiting of interpreters, we staged mock trials to judge whether candidates were able to respond instantly to the verbal stimuli without falling behind. We found that excellent linguists with good academic backgrounds were often unable to react quickly enough and did not qualify. Linguists who proved suitable for simultaneous interpretation tended to have had a substantial stay in the countries of the languages into which or from which they interpreted. I translated from German into English at the English microphone, and my childhood and early adolescence speaking German had been followed by further schooling and employment in England. This gave me a bilingual competence, and since my most recent life experience had been in England, I felt most comfortable interpreting into English.

The task required total concentration, staying in tune with the flow of the speaker, and keeping him or her in sight, to achieve simultaneity. There was a trance-like element in this process. Often when I was asked during a recess what had transpired in the courtroom, I was unable to answer, although I had been on the microphone the entire time.

In interpreting German into English, we faced the peculiarity of the German sentence structure with the verb at the end of a subordinate clause. The longer and more complex the German sentence, and the more erudite the speaker, the further removed the placement of the verb. In English, on the other hand, the verb follows immediately after the noun to anchor the sentence and convey its meaning. These grammatical differences presented a dilemma. If I waited with my interpretation until I heard the verb, the German speaker would have continued with the testimony, and I would fall far behind. The system would break down. Anticipating the verb

before hearing it can be risky, especially during a trial with life or death consequences, and could possibly be prejudicial to the witness or defendant. I found a way around this problem by forming short, independent, and noncommittal sentence fragments from the adverbial clauses preceding the German verb, allowing me to keep up with the speaker. When the verb was finally heard, it would summarize the entire sequence.

Documents submitted during the trials often reflected a deliberately ambiguous use of German to hide incriminating intent—we sometimes called it "Nazi German"—particularly in connection with deportations, concentration camps, and the Holocaust. One well known example is the term "Final Solution," in German *Endlösung*, an innocuous term in itself, but with an intended meaning of extermination as a means of the "solution" to the Jewish problem.

On one occasion my interpretation was challenged by defense counsel when translating the German word *erfassen* to the English verb "seize" in connection with a segment of a population "seized" by German commandos. The defense objected that the term *erfasst* should have been translated as "registered" and not "seized." Indeed, both translations are possible. My choice of "seized" related to the context preceding the sentence. This was an example of deliberate ambiguity in the document to avoid incriminating language. The presiding judge resolved the issue by saying that the record will speak for itself in the total context of the matter.

Another challenge in our task as interpreters related to the difference between spontaneous speech and text read from documents. To be effective and accurate in interpretation, the papers from which counsel or witnesses were reading had to be made available to the interpreters. Without those in front of us, translation would have been extremely difficult.

Counsel and judges required the transcripts of the

proceedings be available as quickly as possible in all four languages. Original testimony was recorded on wire disks, the technology that preceded magnetic tape. Court reporters for German, English, French, and Russian would take down the translation through earphones as it came through their respective channels. Reporters rotated into the courtroom for short fifteen minute "takes," enabling them to transcribe testimony immediately in their offices and make it available to the interpreter for verification and editing. Each interpreting team of twelve would typically work in the courtroom for two ninety-minute sessions per day.

Immediately after leaving the courtroom, the interpreter would check his work, as transcribed by the court reporter, against the original recorded testimony and make any needed corrections. By the end of the day the transcript was available to all counsel and the tribunal in four languages. This process of verification prevented potential errors in the transcript that might have weighty consequences for the defendants and for the outcome of the trials.

The Nuremberg interpreters were a colorful group, coming from a variety of national, linguistic, and professional backgrounds and various parts of the world. They ranged in age from individuals like me in their early twenties to those older —academics, army personnel, and professional conference interpreters. They included several Germans who translated from one of the working languages into German.

An American Army colonel, Leon Dostert, had been raised in France, taught French at Georgetown University, and served as General Eisenhower's interpreter during the war. He had come to Nuremberg as the first chief of the language division, and originated the simultaneous translation concept. He also supervised selection of the interpreting staff.

Serving on the Nuremberg staff from 1945 to 1949, from

In the interpreters' booth (close-up of previous photo).

the first international trial through all subsequent proceedings, I was the interpreter with the longest tenure, and was appointed chief of the interpreting branch during the final two years of the trials, 1947 to 1949.

For the simultaneous interpreter, work at Nuremberg was fascinating, challenging, but also very stressful. We were so preoccupied with our language tasks that we could not easily focus on the substance of the trials. It was only later, with time for perspective, that the substance and meaning of the trials came into sharper focus.

Since the end of the trials, I have spoken and written in the United States and abroad about Nuremberg's pioneering role in establishing the linguistic and technical demands of simultaneous interpretation. This method is now in use at the United Nations and at most international conferences, with the principles and practices taught at universities and special schools in many parts of the world. The pioneering and successful application of simultaneous translating remains one of the important legacies of the Nuremberg trials.

HERMANN GÖRING

As a dominant personality in the dock, Hermann Göring was the leading defendant. Prison diet and discipline seemed to have improved his health, since he was forced to wean himself from a drug dependency. He lost weight and he was mentally alert, as demonstrated by his ability to spar effectively with Chief Prosecutor Robert Jackson during his cross-examination. Göring frustrated Justice Jackson by using lengthy responses to dodge questions and manipulate the cross examination. Jackson's frustration grew when it became evident that Göring had far better mastery of the details and background of Germany's policies, blunting Jackson's probing. I recall a gaffe by Jackson during the cross-examination when he mistakenly referred to Germany's clearing of the "Rhineland territory," when actually installations along the river Rhine were at issue.

When Jackson asked the tribunal to order Göring to respond to his questions with a "yes or no," Lord Justice Lawrence ruled that Göring was entitled to explain his responses. As the cross-examination continued, Jackson lost patience, charging that Göring with his lengthy replies was using the witness stand to indulge in Nazi propaganda and to place himself in a favorable light. From the very beginning of the trial, Göring took it on himself to direct the strategy of his co-defendants by sending notes from the dock to various defense lawyers with suggestions of issues to be raised, questions to be asked, and witnesses to be called. This manipulative behavior became an irritant to the court, and he was ordered to limit his communications to his own defense counsel and to issues pertaining to his own defense. During the trial one of my duties was to check his notes to counsel before they were passed on and to ascertain that

Leading Nazi Hermann Göring.

they were related to his own defense. Göring wanted the German leaders in the dock to present a united front, an aim in which he could not succeed. The disparity among the defendants in their backgrounds and in their roles in relation to Hitler was too great. Such individuals as Hjalmar Schacht, former head of the Reichsbank, or the diplomat Constantin von Neurath would not even deign to speak to such defendants as the Gauleiter Julius Streicher, editor of the virulently anti-Semitic publication *Der Stürmer*, or SS Chief Ernst Kaltenbrunner.

Göring's personal vanity was evident throughout the trial. When testimony was presented about his penchant for luxury or his looting of art works from occupied countries, he became visibly angry, more so than when the larger issues such as his involvement with waging aggressive war and war crimes were the subject during his examination on the stand. He escaped hanging by swallowing a concealed cyanide pill in his cell shortly before his scheduled execution. It is likely that the pill was passed to him by an American officer of the guard whom he had befriended. I recall him sitting in the front row of the dock with a supercilious smile, perhaps knowing that he would cheat the hangman.

ALBERT SPEER

Defendant Albert Speer may have been the most intelligent among Hitler's close entourage. As shown by Speer's writings, self serving to be sure, he came under Hitler's spell as a young architect, flattered and intoxicated by Hitler's trust in him to design grand edifices in Germany. This trust led to his appointment as Minister of Armaments during the war and his role using slave labor and related crimes.

To his credit, he participated in a failed attempt to assassinate Hitler in 1945 and countermanded Hitler's "scorched earth decree" as Allied troops approached Germany, protecting the nation's infrastructure and facilitating postwar recovery. Alhough responsible for forced labor decrees, his anti-Hitler record at the end of the regime and his frank testimony likely saved him from a death sentence and limited his imprisonment to 20 years. When I spoke to him in his cell after sentencing, he fully accepted his guilt and affirmed the validity and significance of the trials as a step to a new future for Germany.

Albert Speer, top Nazi architect and later the Minister of Armaments, crafted settings for many of Hitler's dramatic rallies. Extremely efficient and well-organized, Speer managed to increase Germany's war production even during heavy Allied air bombardment. Although he claimed at the trial not to know about Nazi concentration death camps, Speer used slave labor from the camps to meet his production goals. His organizational genius may have prolonged the war another year.

Nürnberg. Festtribüne auf dem Zeppelinfeld.

RUDOLF HESS

Rudolf Hess and Adolf Hitler pose at the third Nazi Party Congress in Nuremberg in 1927.

During the pretrial phase the case of Deputy Führer Rudolf Hess, stands out. Hess joined Hitler's Munich followers in 1920, became Hitler's private secretary and closest confidant, and eventually, after the Nazis' assumption of power, was designated by Hitler as his deputy. Devoted to Hitler, he was a passionate proponent of Nazi ideology. When studying at the university in Munich, Hess became a protégé of Karl Haushofer, the geopolitician who coined the term *Lebensraum*, living space, a pillar of the Nazi expansionist policy designed to correct perceived injustices of the Versailles Treaty. In the regime's later years, while still in Hitler's entourage, Hess became marginalized when individuals like Hermann Göring and Heinrich Himmler assumed greater influence and power.

In 1941, without Hitler's knowledge or consent, Hess secretly piloted a small plane to Scotland after Germany had planned to open a second front against the Soviet Union. It was a bizarre attempt to contact acquaintances in Great Britain and persuade the British government to join forces with Germany against the Soviet Union. Correctly, as it turned out, he felt that it was a fatal mistake for Germany to fight on two fronts. Hess was interned in England until the end of the war, then sent to Nuremberg to join other accused Nazi leaders. When he arrived in Nuremberg, he claimed total amnesia about his entire past, including his position in Germany, his relationship with Adolf Hitler, and even his family and personal life.

I was closely involved in his interrogations after his arrival in Nuremberg and may shed some light on his behavior and state of mind. The first reaction of the Allied prosecution staff to his claim of amnesia was simply that he was deliberately feigning his loss of memory to avoid prosecution. The pretrial strategy was designed to shock him into acknowledgment of his past and into recognition of his associates. The prosecution gathered several close friends and members of his family, who had not seen him since he flew off to Scotland, and arranged for them to enter the interrogation room, one at a time, and approach Rudolf Hess with the expectation that he would display some reaction and response.

I was present in a corner of the interrogation room, translating to a court reporter what was said by the individuals entering the room and the response by Hess. One of the acquaintances summoned for this encounter was Karl Haushofer, a mentor and close family friend. Haushofer, as well as others, would run up to Hess, embrace him, and exclaim, "Rudolf, Rudolf!" Each time Hess would step back and say: "I wish I could reciprocate your greeting, but I have no memory of knowing you."

Indeed, there was no sign of recognition in his face, nor was there body language that would indicate that these were individuals who had been close to him. Hess would not cooperate with any interrogator, nor with the German defense lawyers assigned to him. As the trial date approached, the prosecution, with the help of psychiatrists brought to Nuremberg, intensified efforts to shock Hess into recovery of his memory. I recall vividly one such effort when Hess was shown a twenty-minute film of newsreels of Nazi party rallies and state functions where he appeared with Hitler, Göring, and others in his dress uniform and full regalia before large crowds. Hess was brought into the projection room where the lights were dimmed with only a bulb illuminating his face.

Serving as interpreter, I asked Hess if he was ready to watch a film. He said: "If it is interesting, I'll watch it." Soon his face appeared on the screen, giving the Hitler salute before roaring crowds. While he had been totally impassive before, this time he reacted strongly, his face tensing up and his hands gripping his chair. When the lights went on, Colonel John Amen, the U.S. interrogator, asked Hess through me if he had any comments. Hess answered: "I was stunned when I heard my name and saw my face on the screen. I cannot comprehend my presence and role in these situations." When his co-defendant Hermann Göring heard about Hess's claim to have lost his memory, he asked for permission to confront him. Brought into an interrogation room where Hess was waiting, Göring said: "Don't you know me? Listen, Hess, I was commandant of the Luftwaffe and later Reichsmarschall. We were together for years." Hess responded: "This is terrible. I don't recognize you. The doctor tells me that my memory will come back." His feigned or real amnesia notwithstanding, Hess was included as one of the defendants in the dock, seated next to Göring in the first row, as the trial started on November 20, 1945.

Medical experts, drawn from the four nations conducting the trial, had concluded that though Hess had an unstable, psychotic personality, he was not insane, and that his condition could be termed a type of hysterical amnesia. At a special hearing before the tribunal a week after the trial started, the defense counsel for Hess claimed that, although Hess could follow the proceedings, his condition of amnesia interfered with his ability to defend himself and that the proceedings against him should be discontinued. At the end of that hearing, as requested by presiding judge Lord Justice Lawrence, Hess made a remarkable statement: "My memory will again respond to the outside world. The reasons for simulating loss of memory were of a tactical nature. I emphasize that I bear full responsibility for everything that I did."

The following day, Lord Justice Lawrence, speaking for the tribunal, declared that the defendant Hess was capable of standing trial and that the motion of defense counsel was denied. As I observed Rudolf Hess in the courtroom during the following months, he displayed intermittent periods of lucidity and engagement with his fellow defendants, followed by longer periods of tuning out. Not wearing earphones, and sitting in the dock with a vacant stare, he seemed to suffer from abdominal cramps and was frequently bent over with a pained expression on his face. Intermittent hysterical amnesia, as described by prison psychiatrist Dr. Gustav Gilbert, may be the best explanation of Hess's condition, recognizing that psychiatry is far from an exact science. Hess was sentenced to life imprisonment, and for a long period was incarcerated in the Spandau prison in Berlin under four-power supervision. In 1987, at the age of ninety-three, Hess committed suicide by self-asphyxiation, tying an electric extension cord around his neck. The last of the international tribunal's defendants to pass on, he had been the solitary inmate at Spandau from 1966 until his death.

MARTIN BORMANN - THE MISSING DEFENDANT

The International Military Tribunal tried twenty-two Nazi leaders, but twenty-seven *should* have been there.

Five of those accused of war crimes escaped trial entirely: Adolf Hitler committed suicide as the war wound down. He was joined in self-inflicted death by Propaganda Minister Joseph Göbbels and Reichsführer SS Heinrich Himmler.

A major Nazi industrialist, Gustav Krupp von Bohlen und Halbach, was ruled medically unfit to stand trial. The leader of the German Labour Front, Robert Ley was captured and indicted, but hanged himself in his cell in October, 1945.

Martin Bormann had vanished, was indicted as the only defendant *in absentia,* found guilty and sentenced to death by hanging. Bormann is remembered as a shadowy figure who was a powerful behind the scenes cog in the wheels of the Nazi regime. He bears responsibility for a key role in the crimes under the Nuremberg indictment.

At the end of the war, Bormann was second only to Hitler himself in the Nazi hierarchy, enjoying the Führer's personal trust. After Rudolf Hess had flown to Great Britain, Bormann had taken his place, had made himself indispensable to the Führer, and had reached a degree of power unequalled by any of the other leading Nazis.

As head of the Party Chancellery and chief aide to Hitler, he controlled access to the Führer and exercised strong influence on policy. He controlled issues of security, legislation, appointments and promotion. Towards the end of the regime he displaced in power such individuals in Hitler's inner circle as Göring, Göbbels and Himmler. Indeed, at Bormann's urging, Göring was dismissed in the spring of 1945 and Himmler's powers were severely curtailed. In the bunker beneath the Berlin chancellery, Bormann signed Hitler's personal testament

USHMM

Martin Bormann ranked just beneath Hitler in the Nazi hierarchy and was in the Führerbunker when Hitler committed suicide. Rumors persisted that Bormann had escaped to a new life in South America like other top Nazis, including Adolf Eichmann and Dr. Josef Mengele. Other reports indicated that he only got just a few blocks from the bunker before being killed.

and watched Hitler kill himself. In the final days preceding the regime's collapse, Bormann transmitted the message to Grand Admiral Karl Dönitz that Dönitz had been appointed successor to the Führer.

None of the Nuremberg defendants had a good word for Bormann, a dislike partially fueled by jealousy of his proximity to Hitler. Speer wrote of Bormann: "Even among so many ruthless men, Bormann stood out by his brutality and coarseness. He had no culture, which might have put some restraint on him. In every case he carried out whatever Hitler ordered."

Another defendant, Hans Fritzsche, one of the three acquitted men in the dock, said of Bormann: "I remember him as the exponent of all the harshest measures in the conduct of the war as well as in domestic and party affairs. Neither in court nor in private talks did I ever hear a single friendly word spoken of this man whose good will had once been so avidly sought."

Bormann's assigned defense counsel, Dr. Friedrich Bergold, had a thankless task. He had no client available to question, and no witnesses willing to testify in Bormann's behalf. The documentary evidence consisted of Martin Bormann's verified signature ordering expulsion, slave labor, and killings of Jews and Slavs, and was unanswerable.

Bormann's fate, after he escaped from the bunker beneath the Reich Chancellery following the Führer's suicide, is still clouded in mystery. Hitler's chauffeur, Erich Kempka, claimed Bormann was killed by an anti-tank shell trying to cross the Russian lines and that he saw Bormann's body. A skeleton discovered in Berlin during excavation may have been his. Others announced Bormann sightings in 1946 in an Italan monastery and later in South America. Although Martin Bormann's final fate remains unclear, in 1973 a West German court formally pronounced him dead.

USHMM

U.S. Assistant Trial Counsel Lt. Thomas F. Lambert, Jr. presents the prosecution's case against Martin Bormann at the International Military Tribunal for war criminals. Bormann was so important a defendant that the Allies prepared and then implemented a complete trial *in absentia*. Witnesses were called, Bormann was represented by a court-appointed defense counsel, and a verdict of guilty and a sentence of death were handed down.

THE TRIBUNAL SETTING

Hermann Göring on the stand. He was extremely opinionated: "The whole conspiracy idea is cockeyed. We had orders to obey the head of state. We weren't a band of criminals meeting in the woods in the dead of night to plan mass murders. The four real conspirators are missing: The Führer, Himmler, Bormann, and Göbbels."

LEFT: The façade of the Palace of Justice. The four flags represent the prosecuting Allied nations, France, the United States, Great Britain and the Soviet Union.

A rare color image of the major defendants in the International War Tribunal. These men were what was left of Nazidom's worst offenders—after the suicides of Adolf Hitler, Joseph Göbbels, Heinrich Himmler, and Robert Ley, and disappearance of Martin Bormann. Left-right: Hermann Goering (slouched), Rudolf Hess, Joachim von Ribbentrop, Wilhelm Keitel, Ernst Kaltenburnner, Alfred Rosenberg, Hans Frank, Wilhelm Frick, Julius Streicher, Walther Funk and Hjalmar Schacht. In the second row are Karl Doenitz, Erich Raeder, Baldur von Schirach, Fritz Saukel, Alfred Jodl, Franz von Papen, Arthur Seyss-Inquart, Albert Speer, Constantin von Neurath and Hans Fritzsche. Sitting in front of them are their defense counsel.

THE MILITARY DEFENDANTS

The military defendants, Generals Keitel and Jodl and Admirals Raeder and Dönitz, both in pretrial interrogations and in testimony during the trial, claimed obedience to Hitler in his capacity as Führer and Commander-in-Chief in response to the charges of conspiring to wage aggressive war and committing war crimes. Their testimony revealed the spell Hitler exercised on them, even when they disagreed with his policies. Keitel mentioned the occasions when he resolved to present objections to Hitler's plans, such as waging a two-front war, but in Hitler's presence was unable to articulate any point of view which differed from that of the Führer.

"Voicing any objection would have been treasonous," he said. This inability to express objections in Hitler's presence, also mentioned by others in his entourage, indicates the hypnotic spell Hitler cast over people, similar to an evangelist at a revival meeting. It was a spell not limited to those in direct contact with him, but extended to the German populace at large. Flags, torchlight parades, and Hitler salutes, all contributed to an atmosphere that swayed and intoxicated the masses.

Colonel General Alfred Jodl, German Chief of Staff under the Dönitz regime that followed Hitler's suicide, signs the unconditional surrender in the SHAEF War Room in Reims, France. Jodl infuriated Eisenhower by delaying signing for two days to allow almost a million German troops along the eastern front to surrender to the Americans rather than the vengeful Russians.

Grand Admiral Erich Raeder expresses his appreciation to the crew of the battle cruiser *Scharnhorst* in April 1942, after their narrow escape through the English Channel. Raeder was a maverick who often opposed Hitler's plans, including Operation Sealion (invading Britain) and Operation Barbarossa (invading the USSR). He eventually resigned his commission in 1943.

Field Marshall Wilhelm Keitel affixing his signature to the ratified surrender terms for the German Army at Russian headquarters in Berlin on May 8, 1945. A cautious officer, Keitel opposed Hitler's invasions of France and Russia. Later he backed down and never disagreed with the Fürher again, earning the sobriquet "nodding donkey" from his colleagues.

Kriegsmarine Commander-in-Chief Admiral Karl Dönitz supervised the secret construction of Germany's U-boat fleet before World War II. He was a strong supporter of Adolf Hitler and was named the Führer's successor on May 2, 1945, serving 23 days as the defeated nation's president. He was found guilty of several of the charges against him at the Nuremberg Trials and was sentenced to ten years in Spandau Prison.

COURTROOM IMPRESSIONS: ATROCITIES ON FILM

The courtroom showing of films of concentration camps, taken by Allied troops as they advanced into Germany, depicted evidence of gas chambers and emaciated survivors, and had a profound impact on the defendants. Many of us on the Nuremberg staff already knew about the Nazi extermination policy through pretrial interrogations and inspections of concentration camps after the war had ended. I had interpreted interrogations of camp commanders and was aware of plans and procedures for deportations and gassings, yet the enormity of the Holocaust with more than six million murdered human beings did not emerge until further evidence came to light.

Court psychiatrist Gustav Gilbert wrote of the agitation among the defendants after the session in which the film on the concentration camps was shown. I was in the courtroom at the time, although no interpretation was necessary, and watched the expressions of horror on the faces of most defendants. In a gesture of defiance, banker Hjalmar Schacht deliberately turned his back to the screen, not wanting to be associated with this evidence. After seeing the footage, Hans Frank, former governor general of Poland, echoed several defendants when he said: "When such atrocities are committed in the name of Germany and the German people, we all bear the guilt of these crimes." While he accepted Germany's guilt, he refused to accept his own personal involvement and specific guilt, despite evidence that Auschwitz and other concentration camps were under his jurisdiction. Defendant Baldur von Schirach, head of the Hitler youth movement, expressed a similar reaction: guilty in a general sense, but not individually involved.

How did I personally react to the depiction of horrors committed by the Nazi regime? Like several other staff members at the trials, I found myself in a dual situation: My function as a tribunal interpreter required a professional attitude that did not allow emotion to affect performance in the courtroom. Despite the fact that I was a witness to and a target of Nazi persecution, experienced the murder of my grandfather, and saw my family forced to escape from Vienna, I focused on my function as a

Josef Oberhauser, Fritz Jirmann, and Kurt Franz outside the Belzec SS Compound. The Belzec Death Camp was notorious and used to experiment in increasing the efficiency of the extermination process.

linguist, responding to the interpretation challenges facing me at the trials. While I was not insensitive to the litany of crimes brought out through documents and testimony, I remained preoccupied with my performance in the courtroom. I did not dwell on my past nor on my personal history. Only later in life, with the benefit of greater reflection and perspective, did I examine the personal implications and legacies of the trials.

A FEW BARELY SURVIVED...OTHERS DIDN'T

April 11, 1945: American troops found rows of workers lying dead on a barracks floor in the German slave labor camp at Nordhausen.

Library of Congress

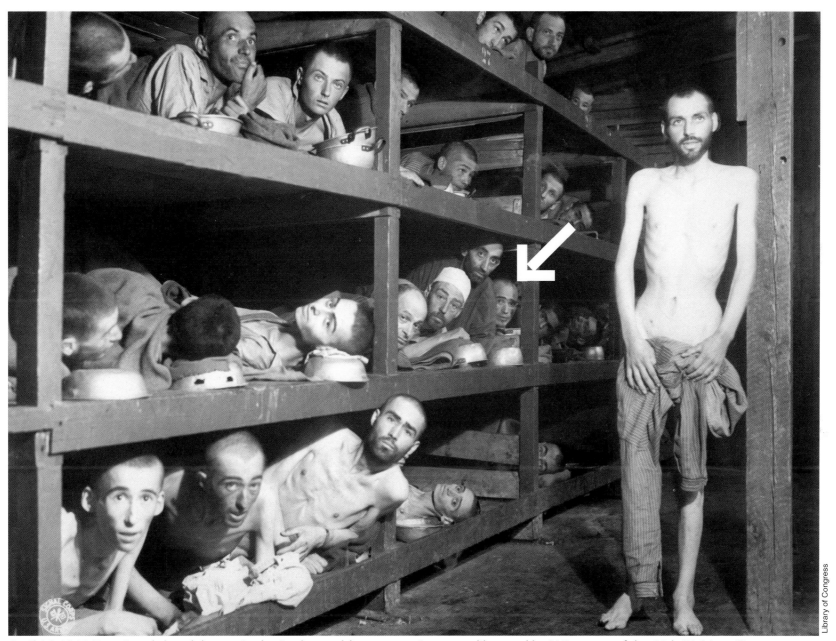

April 16, 1945: Emaciated slave laborers in the Buchenwald concentration camp liberated by U.S. troops of the 80th Division. Sixteen-year-old Elie Wiesel (white arrow) went on to a long career as a writer and activist and was awarded the Nobel Peace Prize in 1986.

THE AMBIANCE OF NUREMBERG

During my time in Nuremberg, cut off from my past, with the future undefined and removed, I had a unique feeling, a heightened sense of the present. Life, in high gear, moved with an intensity that affected the rhythm of work, as well as friendships and contacts. As expressed by the existentialist philosopher Jean Paul Sartre, potential for authentic feeling and behavior rises in times of special events and demanding tasks when the need for a response to challenges intensifies.

For the international staff, life in Nuremberg alternated between work in our offices and in the courtrooms followed by evenings at the city's Grand Hotel. We had the convenience of a motor pool for transportation between the Palace of Justice, our billets, the hotel, and other nearby destinations. The hotel was where the international secretariat, prosecution staff, and press gathered in bars, the dining room, and the ballroom, which featured live music and dancing. There was a surreal aspect to this lifestyle, with the backdrop of the bomb damage and ruins in the old city of Nuremberg adjacent to the hotel, and the grim context of preparations for the trial. There was a food shortage for the German population in the months after the war, and I recall German children pressing their faces against the Grand Hotel's dining room windows where Nuremberg staffers were served opulent meals. The German currency, the mark, had little or no value at the time, causing a "cigarette economy" to develop, where Allied personnel bartered cartons of American cigarettes for such German goods as china or linen and pass them out as tips or favors.

The film *Judgment at Nuremberg* with Spencer Tracy and Marlene Dietrich successfully portrays the moral issues in one of the subsequent trials of Nazi judges where I served frequently as interpreter. The film goes to the heart of what it means to be a judge in a totalitarian state and to individual complicity in executing Nazi law. The film's portrayal of the defendant, a patrician German judge sentencing to death a Jewish man accused of engaging in a relationship with a German woman, embodies the conflict between the rule of law and the rule of man, a theme that runs throughout the Nazi regime and the Nuremberg trials.

The relationship between Spencer Tracy's character as an American judge at the trials, and Marlene Dietrich, the German woman who owned the Nuremberg house he occupied, was pure Hollywood, however, and not at all realistic.

There were indeed liaisons in Nuremberg, but they tended to be among members of the Allied staff and not with German women, particularly where judges and prosecutors were involved. The non-fraternization policy continued during the early years of occupation. As a consequence of the onset of the Cold War, the Soviet delegation, apparently under mandate from Moscow, was ordered not to mix socially with the other delegations, an order which was generally disregarded in the convivial atmosphere of the Grand Hotel. The Soviets tended to be boisterous and enjoyed drinking at the hotel's bar. The French delegation found a gathering place for food and drinks at an inn on the outskirts of Nuremberg that became known as the French Club, which I frequented at times. Another social center on the outskirts of Nuremberg was Stein Castle, headquarters and billets of the Nuremberg press corps, where correspondents from many parts of the world reported on daily developments at the trials. Among the correspondents and authors were Walter Cronkite, reporting for United Press, who later became a television journalist, and Rebecca West, a novelist who wrote for *The New Yorker* magazine.

The main salon of the Grand Hotel in Nuremberg. **INSET:** The Hotel's bar, popular with staff members of the Nuremberg Trials.

Both imsges: Library of Congress

THE CHILLING TESTIMONY OF RUDOLF HÖSS

While Hitler and Himmler meticulously planned the "Final Solution" to eradicate Jews from Europe, it was henchmen like Adolf Eichmann and Rudolf Höss who actually carried it out. Commandant of the Auschwitz death camp, SS Obersturmbannführer Höss was a matter-of-fact murderer, responsible, in his own sworn testimony, for the deaths of some 3,000,000 men, women and children. He notes with some pride how much more efficient his extermination methods were than those used in other death camps.

After the war, Höss evaded capture for more than a year. When the British apprehended him on March 11, 1946—he was betrayed by his wife—Höss was posing as a farmer named Franz Lang. He quickly confessed his true identity.

At Nuremberg, Höss was a witness in the trial of SS Obergruppenführer Ernst Kaltenbrunner, and in the later, separate trials of SS leader Oswald Pohl, and the IG Farben corporation, manufacturer of Zyklon B poison gas. He explained that he had originally expected to put the Auschwitz inmates to work in the Polish farmland. Instead, "I had to go to Himmler in Berlin where he imparted to me the following: 'The Führer has ordered the Final Solution, the *Endlösung*, of the Jewish question. We, the SS, have to execute it.'"

Chief Prosecuter Telford Taylor recollected the profound impact of Höss's testimony at the International Military Tribunal war crimes trial at Nuremberg: "The awful scale of the Nazi terror [inferred from Höss's testimony]—produced by a Führer to whom the defendants had pledged and given their allegiance, and by Himmler, Heydrich, Pohl, Müller, and other leaders of the Nazi government—cast a pall of shame over the defendants and their counsel. No wonder Dr. [Viktor] von der Lippe described the effect of the Höss's testimony as 'crushing' (*niederschmetternd*)."

Höss was eventually turned over to the Polish Supreme National Tribunal for his own trial, where he was sentenced to death and hanged on gallows constructed specifically for his execution near the Auschwitz crematorium.

His confession, which follows, is a chilling indictment of the Nazi regime. I was in the courtroom on a day when Höss testified before the Tribunal and vividly recall his testimony and follow-up interrogation.

Richard Baer, successor to Höss as Commandant of Auschwitz, the notorious Dr. Josef Mengele, who conducted medical experiments on many Auschwitz inmates, and Rudolf Höss socialize at the SS retreat *Solahütte* outside of Auschwitz.

AFFIDAVIT

I, RUDOLF FRANZ FERDINAND HÖSS, being first duly sworn, depose and say as follows:

1. I am forty six years old, and have been a member of the National Socialist Party since 1922; a member of the SS since 1934; a member of the Waffen SS since 1939. I was a member from 1 December 1934 of the SS Guard Unit, the so-called Deathhead Formation (*Totenkopf Verband*).

2. I have been constantly associated with the administration of concentration camps since 1934, serving at Dachau until 1938; then as Adjutant in Sachsenhausen from 1938 to 1 May, 1940, when I was appointed Commandant of Auschwitz. l commanded Auschwitz until 1 December,1943, and estimate that at least 2,500,000 victims were executed and exterminated there by gassing and burning, and at least another half million succumbed to starvation and disease, making a total dead of about 3,000,000. This figure represents about 70% or 80% of all persons sent to Auschwitz as prisoners, the remainder having been selected and used for slave labor in the concentration camp industries. Included among the executed and burnt were approximately 20,000 Russian prisoners of war (previously screened out of Prisoner of War cages by the Gestapo) who were delivered at Auschwitz in Wehrmacht transports operated by regular Wehrmacht officers and men. The remainder of the total number of victims included about 100,000 German Jews, and great numbers of citizens (mostly Jewish) from Holland, France, Belgium, Poland, Hungary, Czechoslovakia, Greece, or other countries. We executed about 400,000 Hungarian Jews alone at Auschwitz in the summer of 1944.

4. Mass executions by gassing commenced during the summer 1941 and continued until fall 1944. I personally supervised executions at Auschwitz until the first of December 1943 and know by reason of my continued duties in the Inspectorate of Concentration Camps that these mass executions continued as stated above. All mass executions by gassing took place under the direct order, supervision and responsibility of Reich Security Office. I received all orders for carrying out these mass executions directly from Reich Security Office.

6. The "final solution" of the Jewish question meant the complete extermination of all Jews in Europe. l was ordered to establish extermination facilities at Auschwitz in June 1941. At that time there were already in the general government three other extermination camps: BELZEK, TREBLINKA and WOLZEK. These camps were under the Einsatzkommando of the

Zyklon-B label from an IG Farben subsidiary, the "German Pest Control Company."

Caution: Poisonous gas.
Zyklon Hydrocyanic Acid
Guarantee of the integrity of this packing enclosure and containment of its contents in storage is valid only for a period of three months beyond the shipment date.
Shipment Date: 25 April 1944
Make every effort to use damaged or decaying containers first. (For example, withdraw and use rusting containers from damp storage environments promptly.)

Security Police and SD. I visited Treblinka to find out how they carried out their exterminations. The Camp Commandant at Treblinka told me that he had liquidated 80,000 in the course of one half year. He was principally concerned with liquidating all the Jews from the Warsaw Ghetto. He used monoxide gas and I did not think that his methods were very efficient. So when I set up the extermination building at Auschwitz, l used Cyclon B, which was a crystallized Prussic Acid which we dropped into the death chamber from a small opening. It took from 3 to 15 minutes to kill the people in the death chamber depending upon climatic conditions. We knew when the people were dead because their screaming stopped. We usually waited about one half hour before we opened the doors and removed the bodies. After the bodies were removed our special commandos took off the rings and extracted the gold from the teeth of the corpses.

7. Another improvement we made over Treblinka was that we built our gas chambers to accommodate 2,000 people at one time, whereas at Treblinka their 10 gas chambers only accommodated 200 people each. The way we selected our victims was as follows: we had two SS doctors on duty at Auschwitz to examine the incoming transports of prisoners. The prisoners

Survivors await evacuation from the Wöbbelin Nazi camp in Ludwigslust, Germany.

would be marched by one of the doctors who would make spot decisions as they walked by. Those who were fit for work were sent into the camp. Others were sent immediately to the extermination plants. Children of tender years were invariably exterminated since by reason of their youth they were unable to work. Still another improvement we made over Treblinka was that at Treblinka the victims almost always knew that they were to be exterminated and at Auschwitz we endeavored to fool the victims into thinking that they were to go through a delousing process. Of course, frequently they realized our true intentions and we sometimes had riots and difficulties due to that fact. Very frequently women would hide their children under the clothes but of course when we found them we would send the children in to be exterminated. We were required to carry out these exterminations in secrecy but of course the foul and nauseating stench from the continuous burning of bodies permeated the entire area and all of the people living in the surrounding communities knew that exterminations were going on at Auschwitz.

8. We received from time to time special prisoners from the local Gestapo office. The SS doctors killed such prisoners by injections of benzine. Doctors had orders to write ordinary death certificates and could put down any reason at all for the cause of death.

9. From time to time we conducted medical experiments on women inmates, including sterilization and experiments relating to cancer. Most of the people who died under these experiments had been already condemned to death by the Gestapo.

10. Rudolf Mildner was the chief of the Gestapo at Kattowicz and as such was head of the political department at Auschwitz which conducted third degree methods of interrogation from approximately March 1941 until September 1943. As such, he frequently sent prisoners to Auschwitz for incarceration or execution. He visited Auschwitz on several occasions. The Gestapo Court, the SS Standgericht, which tried persons accused of various crimes, such as escaping Prisoners of War, etc., frequently met within Auschwitz, and Mildner often attended the trial of such persons, who usually were executed in Auschwitz following their sentence. I showed Mildner throughout the extermination plant at Auschwitz and he was directly interested in it since he had to send the Jews from his territory for execution at Auschwitz.

I understand English as it is written above. The above statements are true; this declaration is made by me voluntarily and without compulsion; after reading over the statement, I have signed and executed the same at Nürnberg, Germany on the fifth day of April 1946.

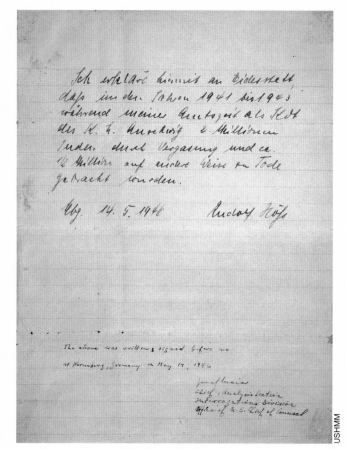

Confession signed by Rudolf Höss. The German text reads: "I declare herewith under oath that in the years 1941 to 1943 during my tenure in office as commandant of Auschwitz Concentration Camp 2 million Jews were put to death by gassing and a 1/2 million by other means. Rudolf Höss. May 14, 1946." The affidavit was witnessed and signed by Josef Maier of the US Chief of Counsel's office.

THE NUREMBERG LEGACY

Considerable analysis of the validity and impact of the Nuremberg trials exists in books and commentaries in law libraries throughout the world. One frequently expressed point of view charges that the Nuremberg trials, as well as the following trials in Tokyo, constituted victor's justice. Here it is important to note that at the time the Nuremberg trial was convened in 1945, Germany as a nation was totally defeated and no German government existed. With the evidence of massive crimes against humanity and millions of victims, it was essential to bring perpetrators to justice without delay. The United Nations, which would have been a preferable convening authority, did not come into existence until a year later. Under these circumstances, an international tribunal consisting of Allied powers was a reasonable and necessary step. Society could not ignore acts of aggression and massive crimes against humanity. The alternative of doing nothing would have been intolerable.

The first two counts of the Nuremberg indictment, accusing Nazi leaders of crimes against peace and of waging aggressive war, were challenged by the defense as constituting so-called *ex post facto law*. How could there be a charge of waging aggressive war, the defense argued, if no codified international body of law exists which defines aggressive war and marks it as a crime? Indeed, this question continues to be raised at the present time in connection with the charter of the International Criminal Court at the Hague, which has not reached agreement among the signatories on the issue of defining aggressive war. In responding to the *ex post facto* defense argument, the Nuremberg prosecution countered that principles of natural law operate underlying codified law. Furthermore, the prosecution argued that international agreements enacted prior to World War II, such as the Kellogg-Briand Pact, to which Germany was a signatory, established aggressive wars as violating international covenants. This pact, a key multilateral treaty, "binds the signatories to respect international norms to maintain peace and forbids the threat or use of military force in contravention of international law." Consequently the Nuremberg tribunal upheld the count of crimes against peace, finding many of the accused guilty under the charge of waging aggressive war.

Counts three and four of the indictment, the commission of war crimes and crimes against humanity, were supported by overwhelming and indisputable evidence through documents, testimony by victims and witnesses, and the physical evidence of gassing and annihilation at concentration camps. In the defense against these counts there could be no denial that such atrocities took place. The key defense approach, largely countered by incriminating evidence, was that the accused had no knowledge of or was not involved in these crimes.

An undercurrent running through the revelations at the trials raised a fundamental question: how was it possible for such atrocities to be committed in the name of Germany, a nation with a rich cultural tradition in literature, science, and the arts, a pillar of European civilization? As members of the Nuremberg staff placed close to the evidence, we raised this question, as did the world community at large, which encountered reports of atrocities through the media.

In the years after the trials, when asked to speak or write about Nuremberg, I responded to this question by extending it beyond Germany and giving it a universal significance. When checks on governmental power and control do not exist, when a dictatorship disregards and nullifies existing laws and creates its own decrees, when the achievement of a desired end for a nation justifies any means to obtain it, when persecution of segments of a population becomes government

NIGHT OF THE EXECUTIONS

The night of the Nuremberg executions, October 16, 1946, remains a vivid memory. As a staff member of the International Military Tribunal, I knew the executions were to take place that night, though the specific time was not revealed. They were carried out in a gymnasium adjacent to the prison cells, where scaffolds were erected the day before. Several official witnesses representing the tribunal and selected members of the international press corps attended and reported on the executions.

All witnesses, including the press, were ordered to the site earlier that evening and were not allowed to communicate with the outside or leave the prison until the following morning. Though I had no access to the execution site, I remained in my office at the Palace of Justice along with other staffers and observers.

This news blackout resulted in an embarrassing gaffe committed by several European newspapers. In a rush to capture the story, banner headlines on the morning of October 16 proclaimed that eleven defendants were hanged, though in fact Göring had committed suicide in his cell by swallowing a cyanide pill about two hours before he was to be led to the gallows. The time difference between Europe and the United States spared the American press from the same mistake. After the executions, Göring's body was taken to the gymnasium and placed beside the other ten, so his death could be officially certified. Although there are many theories, one implicating an American officer of the guard who was close to Göring, it has never been proven conclusively how he got hold of the cyanide.

On the day following the executions, the bodies were cremated and the ashes strewn in a river.

US Army hangman, MSgt John C. Woods, bungled the executions by not assuring immediate death. Several of the condemned men strangled to death while dangling from the rope.

National Archives and Records Administration

policy, and when the world community fails to react to crimes being committed by a dictatorship, the result leads to the abyss into which Germany descended during the Nazi era. In this sense the Nuremberg legacy, as a cornerstone of international law, takes on a universal significance beyond the role of Germany during the Hitler regime.

As for the German man and woman in the street, their support of the Nazi regime must be seen in the context of Germany's struggle for survival during wartime and living under the pressure of a dictatorship where dissent had harsh, even fatal consequences. Nevertheless, isolated and heroic examples exist of German resistance to the Nazis. The failed July 20, 1944 plot to assassinate Hitler, led by Claus von Stauffenberg, stands out as a courageous attempt which, had it succeeded, would have hastened the end of the war and influenced postwar policies and attitudes affecting Germany. There were other, less well known, stands of defiance.

The question of the average German's knowledge about ongoing deportations, killings, and gassings, let alone shared guilt and complicity, continues to be asked. In his controversial book, *Hitler's Willing Executioners*, political scientist Daniel Goldhagen draws a strong causal relationship between anti-Semitism and the persecution and extermination of Jews, to which many ordinary Germans contributed and supported. His attribution of collective German guilt, however, fails to take into account the silent segment of the German population unable, and also often unwilling, to raise their voices in an atmosphere of a cruel and punitive dictatorship.

From my perspective, living for several postwar years among Germans, I came to understand this silent segment of the German population, seeing themselves also as victims of the Nazi regime. And I came to appreciate the decency of many of my German neighbors and friends.

THE "JULY PLOT" TO KILL HITLER

An account of Nazi atrocities from 1933 to 1945 requires recognition of heroic instances of resistance within Germany. Sources and methods of resistance varied. They ranged from the Solf Circle, an informal gathering of intellectuals in Berlin, many of whom were arrested, tortured and executed, to the White Rose student group, originating at the University of Munich, who launched an anti-Nazi leaflet campaign.

National Archives and Records Administration

Claus von Stauffenberg (far left) with Adolf Hitler (right).

When the tide of war turned in favor of the Allies in 1944, several senior German military officers met secretly to plan ways to bring down Hitler's regime, realizing that the Führer's irrational military decisions were leading to Germany's ruin. They hatched a plot to assassinate Hitler and end the war. Conspirator Claus von Stauffenberg volunteered to plant a bomb at a July 20, 1944 meeting at which Hitler was present. The bomb (in von Stauffenberg's briefcase) detonated, killing four men in the hut. None of them, unfortunately, was Adolf Hitler, who was injured but survived.

The conspirators were rounded up and swiftly dispatched. Von Stauffenberg was shot by firing squad in the courtyard of the War Ministry on Bendlerstrasse in Berlin. It was later reported that just before the fatal shots rang out, he shouted, "Long live our sacred Germany." After the war, Claus von Stauffenberg became a German national hero, and the street on which he was executed was renamed Stauffenbergstrasse.

Each of the four powers provided a judge and an alternate on the International Military Tribunal. The top row, left to right: alternate Lt. Col. Alexander Volchkov, Judge (and Major General) Iona Nikitchenko, both USSR, and alternate Sir Norman Birkett and presiding Judge Sir Geoffrey Lawrence of Great Britain. Not pictured seated to the right of the photo: Alternate Judge Norman Birkett of Great Britain, Judges Francis Biddle and John J. Parker of the United States, and Judges Henri Donnedieu de Vabres and Robert Falco of France. I am seated second from right in middle row, acting in another of my roles as language aide to court reporters, assisting with German terminology.

TWELVE SUBSEQUENT PROCEEDINGS

Following the major international trial, twelve lesser trials were held in Nuremberg, prosecuted by the United States alone. The U.S. military court conducted the trials in the same courtroom as the previous International Tribunal. Defendants included physicians who performed forced medical experiments, Nazi judges, governmental and military leaders, execution commandos, industrialists, and ministers who carried out criminal policies. Many of these involved capital crimes where the death penalty was meted out.

I stayed on in Nuremberg throughout these trials, serving as chief of the interpreting branch from 1947 to 1949. The later trials were prosecuted by Brigadier General Telford Taylor, a key associate of Justice Jackson during the international trial. Taylor later became a distinguished law professor and author at Columbia University.

During these trials, Germany's role in U.S. foreign policy evolved from that of a defeated enemy to becoming a crucial ally in the Cold War and a bulwark in the defense against the Soviet Union. Amnesties and reduction of sentences given at that time appear in the light of a changing American stance toward Germany. There was an underlying tension between the Nuremberg mission of bringing war criminals to justice and the political and strategic reality of embracing Germany as a partner.

Of course, this was not an "either or" scenario. Enlightened German postwar opinion, characterized by such figures as prime minister Konrad Adenauer willingly drew a strong line behind the past, rejecting the Nazi era and recognizing guilt. Determined to start the postwar period with a clean slate, Germany was looking forward to democracy, and the rule of law, leading eventually to membership in NATO and the European Union.

THE MEDICAL TRIAL

One of my tasks was interpretation during the trial of Nazi doctors accused of conducting forced medical experiments on concentration camp inmates. Polish female ex-prisoners, brought to Nuremberg as witnesses, testified to the artificial induction of gangrene infections on their bodies in order to test the effectiveness of new drugs. The consequences included losses of limbs and frequently losses of life.

Other experiments on camp inmates involved immersion in seawater, exposure at high altitude, freezing, exposing victims to poison gas and infecting victims with malaria, typhus, and tuberculosis. Defendants in the medical dock included physicians of high reputation, some known in medical communities beyond Germany. Given they had been in a healing profession, the evidence of their involvement in such crimes proved particularly shocking. While they claimed that their experiments aimed to advance medical knowledge and ultimately save lives, follow-up studies revealed that not a single medical discovery of any importance could be traced back to these experiments. It was a case of ends justifying any means, a pervasive theme running through all the trials.

During the medical trial, the unfamiliar terminology and technical testimony posed challenges for us. Much of this terminology was based on Latin roots, common to both German and English languages, consequently our task as interpreters, lacking medical backgrounds, required supplying appropriate English or German pronunciation to the Latin stems.

The lead defendant in the doctors' trial was Dr. Karl Brandt, chief health commissioner for the Reich. He was ultimately responsible for the forced medical experiments as well as the Nazi euthanasia program, designed to eliminate "undesirables." Well spoken and intelligent, Brandt also acted as Hitler's personal escort physician. In many respects architect Albert

Speer and physician Brandt had much in common: both were fairly young, bright, and ambitious, flattered and blinded by Hitler's confidence in them, and by their placement in his close entourage.

I recall an interesting encounter with one of the defendant doctors. I had an obstinate skin irritation on my face that would not clear up despite an ointment from the dispensary. During a recess one of the doctors beckoned to me and asked me to approach the dock. He looked at my face, scribbled a prescription on a piece of paper, and suggested that I obtain the medication at a Nuremberg pharmacy. He said to me that if I applied that salve twice a day it would take care of the skin problem. I thought, "Why not give it a try?" and went to the pharmacy, where it was verified as a bona fide medication. Lo and behold, within a few days the irritation was gone! I mention this to point out that many of these defendants, while they displayed a disregard for human life and a violation of medical ethics during the Nazi regime, also came across as educated and polite individuals with whom you would easily socialize under normal conditions. This dualism, the horrible crimes and the impact of educated professionals, was difficult to reconcile.

The Doctors' Trial

Twenty-one of the 23 defendants were physicians. (Viktor Brack and Wolfram Sievers were Nazi SS officials.) All were accused of having been involved in Nazi human experiments. Of the 23, seven were executed, nine received long prison sentences and seven were acquitted. The faces of the guilty are pictured below along with their original court sentences:

Wilhelm Beiglboeck
15 years in Prison

Viktor Brack
Hanged

Karl Brandt
Hanged

Rudolf Brandt
Hanged

Hermann
Brecker-Freyseng
20 years in Prison

Fritz Fischer
Life in Prison

Karl Gebhardt
Hanged

Karl Genzken
Life in Prison

Siegfried Handloser
Life in Prison

Waldemar Hoven
Hanged

Joachim Mrugowsky
Hanged

Herta Oberheuser
20 years in Prison

Helmut Poppendick
10 years in Prison

Gerhard Rose
Life in Prison

Oskar Schroeder
Life in Prison

Wolfram Sievers
Hanged

NUREMBERG SNAPSHOTS

With Pi'ilani at our Darmbach billet.

Pi'ilani wrote on the back of this photo: "The steeples are about all that's left of what used to be a beautiful Lutheran church. I'm standing on the lawn of a former Luftwaffe office."

Working on a transcript in my Palace of Justice office.

General Telford Taylor, chief prosecutor at the subsequent trials.

At our Darmbach (Nuremberg outskirts) garden with Pascha, our dachshund. Later he was with us aboard the freighter crossing the Atlantic and came with us to Hawai'i.

The Sterner family, our German neighbors adjoining our Darmbach house. From left to right: Else Sterner (mother), Christa Sterner, younger daughter, Hansfried Sterner, son, and Lieselotte Sterner, older daughter, who was to stay with us later in Hawai'i.

Court reporters dinner in Nuremberg. Pi'ilani and I are seated fourth and fifth from left.

NUREMBERG FRIENDSHIPS

Life in Nuremberg consisted of work under intense pressure in the courtrooms, interspersed with welcome weekend trips to the Alps and travel to various destinations in Europe during trial recesses. A bonus of the assignment to Nuremberg was the opportunity for free flights aboard military aircraft on a space-available basis.

In summers I frequently attended the Salzburg Music Festival in company with other Nuremberg staffers, and in winters we often drove to ski lodges in the Garmisch and Berchtesgaden mountains. After the initial period of stay at the Grand Hotel, I moved into lodgings at Darmbach, a residential suburb of Nuremberg, where I shared a house with several colleagues on the Nuremberg staff. At Darmbach I befriended a neighboring German family, the Sterners, a kind and convivial couple with three children, two girls and a boy, an encounter which grew into a close friendship continuing to this day. Indeed, the older girl, Lieselotte (or Lilo as we called her), was later to come to Hawai'i, stay with us, and become part of the Ramler's extended family.

My circle of friends in Nuremberg included colleagues among interpreters and translators, court reporters, lawyers, and journalists—a stimulating group that enriched the time at Nuremberg both professionally and socially.

Revisiting the Sterner family after the trials, I pose with Lieselotte Sterner. Lilo eventually joined us in Hawai'i for several years and now lives in Tahiti.

MEETING PIʻILANI

When I reflect on the personal impact of Nuremberg, I am struck by the power and consequence of an encounter which was to influence the course of my life. I met Piʻilani Ahuna at the Palace of Justice soon after she had arrived from the United States, slated to be assigned to the court reporting staff. Born and raised in Hawaiʻi, she had finished her college studies in California, where she also acquired court reporting skills. While working at a San Francisco law firm, she heard about the need for court reporters at the Nuremberg trials, submitted an application, was assigned, and made her way to Germany.

Perhaps the first spark of attraction was ignited by her arresting appearance and by the impact of an attractive and shapely Hawaiian-Chinese young woman in a WAC uniform entering the courtroom with her stenograph pad.

Court reporters, assigned at the trials to take testimony in each of the four working languages, would take turns sitting in the courtroom in the tier below the judges' bench, earphones tuned to the interpretation into their language—German, English, French, or Russian. One of my duties at the trials, related to interpretation, was to check the English transcript drafts for accuracy in the transcription of German proper names, places, and ranks unfamiliar to court reporters.

When Piʻilani first entered the courtroom, she caused a noticeable buzz among defendants. As I looked over to the dock, I noticed their curiosity about her ethnic identity. I could just imagine a defendant asking his neighbor in the dock: "Where do you think she comes from?"

Piʻilani and I soon became friends, enjoyed the sharing of our diverse backgrounds, and, perhaps inevitably, fell in love. We would have dinner together, spend weekends walking in the woods in the outskirts of Nuremberg, and go on excursions in the Alps when the trials were in recess. With her hailing from Hawaiʻi and my background from Vienna and London, Piʻilani and I had much to share: her fascinating stories about Hawaiian life and Pacific cultures, and my role in introducing her to European experiences beyond the courtroom and the occupation setting. Our relationship included our wider circle of friends, particularly among court reporters, interpreters, and correspondents, often sharing meals and weekend activities.

Among the correspondents was Alfred Kornfeld, a young New Yorker covering the trials for *Time* magazine. Alfred, intelligent and dashing, soon became a good friend and joined us in many of our activities. It came as quite a surprise, not long after we had met Alfred, when Piʻilani told me that Alfred had proposed to her and had suggested marriage in Nuremberg. Following his father's footsteps, Alfred planned to enter the publishing business after his stint as a correspondent and wanted to build his future with Piʻilani.

Piʻilani faced a dilemma. While we had strong feelings for each other, marriage was not in our plans. I told Piʻilani during our many talks that she should seriously consider accepting Alfred's proposal. He was a man with strong plans for the future, he was congenial and intelligent, and they would make a fine couple. On the other hand, as much as I was devoted to Piʻilani, I told her that I did not feel ready for marriage and that I felt too unsettled to contemplate such a commitment. For many days Piʻilani agonized over the decision, discussing her feelings with Dorothy Fitzgerald, another court reporter and close friend, and finally agreed to marry Alfred.

The engagement was announced and plans were made for a wedding at the Stein castle, the headquarters and residence of the Nuremberg press corps. Together with Dorothy and

PI'ILANI AT WORK IN NUREMBERG

March 22, 1946: Top Nazi defendant Herman Göring in the witness chair. Pi'ilani (circled) takes Göring's testimony. Our friendship was to blossom into marriage.

American soldiers stand suicide watch outside each cell in Nuremberg Prison, where defendants standing trial before the International Military Tribunal were incarcerated. This practice was instituted after defendant Robert Ley killed himself—he cut a towel into strips for a noose, fastened it to a toilet pipe and strangled himself. Prisoners were allowed only a single spoon to eat and that was confiscated immediately after each meal. Believing that hanging was beneath a man of his stature, Hermann Göring somehow acquired a cyanide capsule and crunched it in his teeth shortly before his scheduled execution. Guards were unable to get into his cell because the keys were kept elsewhere, and Göring died before they could save him. He left a note for Allied authorities: "I would have had no objection to being shot. I will not facilitate execution of Germany's Reichsmarschall by hanging! For the sake of Germany, I cannot permit this.... For this reason, I have chosen to die like the great Hannibal."

several of Pi'ilani's friends, I helped with arrangements for the wedding, including the invitations, the ceremony, and music by an ensemble of the Nuremberg symphony orchestra. I remember the wedding dinner in a private dining room of the Stein castle, seated at a table next to Pi'ilani and Alfred.

In retrospect their marriage would appear to be a painful experience for me, the loss of a woman I loved. However, at the time I was convinced that this marriage was the right decision for Pi'ilani and good for her future.

Alfred's *Time* assignments took him beyond Nuremberg to other areas in Germany while Pi'ilani continued with her court reporting duties at the trials.

A few weeks after the wedding, several of us in their circle of friends arranged a post-wedding party at the Nuremberg Grand Hotel, where we would gather for dinner and dancing. Alfred was due back from an assignment in Berlin to join us for the party. When he did not show up in time, we went ahead with dinner. Later, when the group was on the dance floor, a hotel clerk called me to the telephone. The shocking message from the police indicated that while driving on the Autobahn, Alfred had collided with a truck and died instantly.

I called Dorothy out of the ballroom to find a way to inform Pi'ilani, who was on the dance floor. We contacted an army chaplain, and asked him to come immediately to the hotel and wait in an empty room. We took Pi'ilani to see him, telling that an urgent personal message awaited her. Pi'ilani told me later that as soon as she saw the cross on the officer's collar, she knew that something terrible had happened to Alfred.

I helped Pi'ilani with arrangements to notify Alfred's family and fly his body from Berlin to New York. Pi'ilani

Pi'ilani and Alfred Kornfeld next to his *Time* magazine press car.

left her job in Nuremberg, called on Alfred's family, and then returned to her home in Hawai'i. Understandably she was restless, found it hard to settle down, and decided to return to Europe in the company of Dorothy Fitzgerald to study French, first in Switzerland and then in Paris.

I stayed in touch from Nuremberg, frequently taking the Orient Express train to Paris to visit her. I would board a sleeper compartment of the train in Nuremberg on a Friday afternoon and arrive in Paris the following morning, returning to Nuremberg on Sunday evening. Together with my passport, I would give the train conductor a generous tip, so I would not be awakened when the train stopped at the French border at night. In Paris Pi'ilani stayed in a small hotel at Rue Jacob, in the Latin Quarter, not far from the Sorbonne and the cafes of the Boulevard Saint-Germain.

Parisian weekends with Pi'ilani had a special quality, enhanced by the setting at the Left Bank; there were strolls along the Seine, baguettes and croissants in the morning, and aperitifs before a leisurely bistro dinner in the evening. We visited museums and galleries, climbed up to the cathedral atop Montmartre, and savored our bond with the City of Light as our backdrop. For me these weekends meant a dual love affair with Pi'ilani and Paris.

Indeed, my interest in French culture and language was sparked during those days, to be continued and nurtured in the years ahead, with study periods and stays in France to follow in my later career.

My relationship with Pi'ilani by this time had become more focused, more mature, deepened by the trauma of Alfred's death and the passage of time, and we decided to get married. Our simple wedding, performed in Paris at the town hall of the sixth arrondissement in the Latin Quarter, had just two witnesses, both Nuremberg friends, a British correspondent

with the Reuters agency and a *Life* magazine photographer. Dorothy Fitzgerald was with us as we toasted the wedding at the Georges V hotel bar along the Champs Elysee before Pi'ilani and I crossed the channel to London for a very brief honeymoon. My duties in Nuremberg did not allow for an extended absence.

After clearing some bureaucratic hurdles, Pi'ilani managed to get rehired as court reporter for the additional Nuremberg trials. We were assigned a comfortable house in the Darmbach suburb of Nuremberg and began our first year of married life under conditions marked by a Germany still under Allied occupation and by our duties at the trial.

Pi'ilani showed her talents as homemaker and decorator by creating an attractive environment with paintings, knick knacks, and items of furniture. While we worked hard, we also enjoyed comforts unusual for a young married couple. We acquired a new American automobile, a red Ford sedan, which we picked up in Holland at The Hague and drove to Nuremberg. We obtained the services of a driver, as well as a maid, to maintain our household. Both were to remain with us until the end of our duties in Germany.

Reaching out as a warm and spirited hostess, Pi'ilani would invite fellow staff members to our house for dinners and informal parties. We also befriended German neighbors who would drop by the house for visits, especially the Sterners, who in future years became part of our extended family. The army PX and commissary were available to us for shopping, supplemented by local purchases such as fresh fruits and vegetables, as these items became available after the end of the war. During the period of severe shortages at war's end, much of the economy was based on barter, when cigarettes or American canned or packaged food stuffs could be exchanged for fresh produce.

The author is at lower right leaning against the railing aboard the ship *Cape Mohican*. The ship is crossing the Atlantic from Hamburg to New York at the conclusion of the Nuremberg trials in the summer of 1949. The two men with the author in the photo are crew members. The *Cape Mohican* had been a Merchant Marine vessel operating in the Mediterranean Sea and Atlantic Ocean during World War II. After the war, she became a civilian freighter carrying just twelve passengers along with her cargo.

AFTER NUREMBERG: TRAVEL TO HAWAI'I

When the trials came to an end, we faced decisions for our future. Opportunities existed to work in Germany as civil servants with the U.S. occupation, again under comfortable conditions, but we resisted the temptation. We realized that we needed to establish roots and face the reality of a normal life, although it was not clear to us yet where and how such a life would take shape. As a first step, Pi'ilani insisted that she would introduce me to Hawai'i, to her family, and to a taste of Hawaiian lifestyle and culture. I was ready to move on and to take the next steps toward a yet undefined future life.

At the conclusion of the last trial in 1949, our driver took us to Hamburg to embark on the Atlantic crossing to New York's Staten Island, aboard a freighter carrying only twelve passengers. We took along our dachshund, Pasha, who soon became a favorite of passengers and crew. Similar to my crossing of the English Channel from Vienna to London, this trip was the beginning of a new chapter in my life, taking me from Europe to the United States, and particularly to Hawai'i, then still a U.S. territory prior to joining the union in 1959.

In New York we took delivery of a new automobile for a leisurely drive across the United States, a three-month road trip that allowed us to visit friends living in various parts of the U.S. who had been in Nuremberg with us. We made many scenic stops, including the Rocky Mountains, the Grand Canyon, and California's Pacific coast. For me this was an impressive introduction to the size and diversity of the United States, as well as to the friendly spirit of Americans we encountered at tourist sites, motels, and coffee shops.

Beyond the vast panorama of America, I was struck by the relaxed mood of Americans we met during the drive across country. Coming from Europe and its stratified society, I was impressed by the egalitarian spirit prevailing everywhere, by

We arrive in Hawai'i.

folksy greetings extended to us, and by the informality all around us. Americans take this spirit for granted, as I do now, but at that time it was quite a revelation.

We planned to cross from San Francisco to Hawai'i aboard the *Lurline*, but a longshoremen's strike had halted all ocean travel to the islands. Instead we took an an eleven hour flight on a double-decker Pan American Stratocruiser. The night flight's length was well compensated, however, by elegant dinner service, comfortable bunks on the upper deck, and breakfast served before arrival in Hawai'i. Flying has certainly changed since those days.

4

HAWAI'I
1949-present

In Honolulu we were met by Pi'ilani's parents, Moses and Annie Ahuna, in a spirit of Hawaiian hospitality at its best. They had rented an apartment for us, stocked the refrigerator, and introduced the European *haole* (stranger) to Honolulu members of the Ahuna clan before taking us on a visit to the Ahuna homestead on the island of Hawai'i, commonly called the Big Island. Well known and respected on the Big Island, Pi'ilani's father had retired as chief engineer of the island's former railroad system and then served as an expert on native crops, and a grower and distributor of Hawaiian medicinal plants. In later years he became an adjunct lecturer on these plants for community colleges throughout the islands.

As a Big Island patriarch, Moses Ahuna exerted a strong influence on his grandchildren, transmitting to them a strong feeling for Hawaiian identity and culture. He opposed affirmative action policies for Hawaiians—despite historical injustices—feeling strongly that Hawaiians needed to be self-sufficient and earn their rewards through hard work. He surrounded himself with many residents of Japanese ancestry who elected him "farmer of the year."

Pi'ilani's mother taught at Keaukaha Elementary School in Hilo, and with Moses, had a strong commitment to community service. As the oldest daughter of six children, Pi'ilani distinguished herself by her adventurous spirit, leading her to Germany and the Nuremberg trials. Her father took me around the Big Island and impressed me with his vast knowledge of the topography and ecosystem of the islands, able to identify by date of origin each lava flow on the island. While he did not enter politics himself, he was an advisor and campaign manager of several candidates.

At first we intended to visit the islands for a few months before taking up residence on the U.S. mainland or possibly in England. I could not imagine a life and career for us on one of the tiny specks of islands in mid-Pacific. Certainly it had lush scenery and welcoming people, but wouldn't I be cut off from the world? Soon, however, I began to see that Hawai'i combined its Polynesian roots and identity with strong American influences. Far from isolated, Hawai'i was a crossroads of the Pacific with good access to communications and news. I was soon attracted to the multiethnic population and diversity of cultures. To me, Hawai'i embodied a coming together of ethnic groups, with the welcoming spirit of the host Polynesian culture creating an *'ohana*, the Hawaiian term for family and community spirit.

Pi'ilani's parents, Annie and Moses Ahuna at the family home in Hilo on the island of Hawai'i.

Honolulu Harbor in 1850. Although pictured here about a century before Pi'ilani and I arrived to make our home, the Islands were already a center of international commerce. Punahou School, where I would spend over four decades, had been established in 1841. The whaling trade was then in full swing, with Hawai'i at its Pacific epicenter. It would shortly be followed by sugar, pineapple, and later, visitors.

Despite its history of warring Polynesian chiefdoms and the overthrow and annexation of the kingdom by the United States, Hawai'i remains an example of social harmony, an island community where different cultures coexist peacefully and where diversity can be embraced.

No doubt my interest in exploring cultures of the Pacific and Asia regions was sparked by these early experiences, which led to my commitment to teaching, community service, and travel in the region. One of my priorities was to continue my interrupted education by earning a graduate degree. Honolulu had a large university with interesting and diverse programs in advanced studies, with special strength in Pacific and Asian languages and cultures. All these advantages combined to convince us to stay in Hawai'i, with Pi'ilani taking a job in the court system of the Pearl Harbor Naval District while I enrolled at the University of Hawai'i.

I included an elementary course in Mandarin Chinese in my studies at the university, unaware that I would have intensive contacts with China later in life. Joining the debate club at the university, I developed strong friendships among fellow debaters, one of whom was to become mayor of the Big Island. Another debater and I represented the University of Hawai'i on a debating trip to several universities on the U.S. mainland. He would later become a Hawai'i Supreme Court judge. Speaking for the affirmative side, our debate proposition advocated that the United States establish economic and security alliances with nations of the Pacific, somewhat analogous to NATO in Europe.

In hindsight, Pacific economic and security alliances as a topic proved prescient. China's Communist revolution had recently taken place, the Korean War had started, U.S. forces still occupied Japan, and Asia was transforming.

With headquarters of the Pacific military command at Pearl Harbor, Hawai'i's position influenced U.S. strategy and defense. The Cold War, with Asia playing a strong role, dominated international relations. Far from isolated, Hawai'i was in the mainstream of events.

Often I was invited by community organizations in Honolulu to speak about my experience at the Nuremberg trials or about issues pertaining to Europe.

A Honolulu radio station asked me to collaborate on a series of commentaries on international personalities and events, requiring me to prepare copy for broadcasts, actually monologues, under deadline pressure. These radio commentaries offered far more length and depth than would be possible today, when sound bites dominate television news.

My course work at the university, focusing on political science topics, led to a thesis entitled "The MacArthur Constitution: A Study of Japanese Attitudes towards Revision." This study represented the beginning of my interest in developments in Japan, an interest which grew in intensity and continues strongly to this day.

Interestingly, the issue of constitutional revision, now more than five decades later, still plays a central role in Japanese politics.

Having experienced the postwar conditions and the occupation of Germany, I could see both analogies and contrasts in Japan, making it a fertile area for exploration. Both countries rejected militaristic dictatorship and the policies of aggression leading to the World War II. Both countries formed democratic governments. The Tokyo trials of Japan's wartime military and political leaders, based on the Nuremberg charter and precedent, followed one year after Nuremberg and resulted in a similar range of judgments and sentences.

Germany's total repudiation of the Hitler regime, however, represented a stronger break with the past than was the case in Japan. In contrast to Germany, in Japan there was greater continuity with its past history, especially since Japan's infrastructure at the end of the war, despite the bombings of Hiroshima and Nagasaki, remained generally intact. The emperor system, albeit with renunciation of the emperor's divinity status, continued under the postwar constitution in the interest of Japan's stability and historical continuity. At war's end many economic and political leaders resumed their previous functions.

Japan's attitudes about its history leading up to and during World War II continue as issues to the present time, especially with the controversial visits by Japanese political leaders to the Yasukuni Shinto shrine, where several convicted war criminals are buried. Japan's disputed compensation to Korean "comfort women," forced into sexual slavery during the war, causes continuing tensions in Korean-Japanese relationships. It may take another Japanese generation before these issues are resolved.

Joining the Punahou School faculty in 1951, opens for me a vocation in education and community service with one of Hawaii's venerable institutions. Old School Hall, built in 1852, still functions as a classroom building in the center of the 76-acre campus. Punahou, translated from the Hawaiian language as "new spring", was founded by New England missionaries in 1841 to educate their children. Over the decades the student body, reflecting Hawaii's multi-ethnic mix, has expanded to 3700 students in its elementary and secondary divisions. Offering a rigorous and extensive college preparatory curriculum and diverse offerings in the arts and athletics, Punahou ranks among the outstanding private schools in the United States. In its May 2008 issue, the Sports Illustrated magazine rated Punahou's athletic program as the top in the United States.

JOINING THE PUNAHOU SCHOOL FACULTY

While studying at the University of Hawai'i, I was contacted by the principal of Punahou School, who asked me if I would accept a part-time position starting the following semester teaching elementary German. As was the case in many schools throughout the United States, the teaching of German had been discontinued because of the war and was now being reinstated. I thought that a teaching stint would be an enjoyable challenge and accepted the offer.

Punahou has an attractive campus at the mouth of O'ahu's Manoa Valley, featuring large playing fields, handsome buildings (some of which date back to the 19th century), and excellent athletic facilities. Founded by Protestant missionaries in 1841, Punahou grew into one the largest independent schools in the United States. It enjoyed a reputation for high quality college preparatory education. We were offered faculty housing on campus, enjoying subsidized rent and a close walking distance to my classes.

Soon the Punahou experience became much more than a job. I enjoyed the daily contact with enthusiastic students, stimulating colleagues, and the challenge and satisfaction of teaching. Asked if I would agree to continue teaching full time at Punahou in the following year, adding French to my teaching assignments, I realized that I had found my vocation. I signed the contract and began what was to become a forty-four year career, linked to a great educational institution with deep roots in Hawai'i's history and community.

Given the impact of New England missionaries in the founding of the school, Punahou shares characteristics with traditional New England prep schools such as Andover and Exeter. I have come to appreciate Punahou's role in transmitting to students an ethos and loyalty springing from the school's long tradition.

Under the leadership of President John Fox, Punahou opened its admissions policy, changing from a predominantly caucasian student body to a school population fully reflecting the ethnic diversity of Hawai'i. This diversity continued, even increased, under the tenures of President Fox's successors, Dr. Roderick McPhee and Dr. James Scott.

Dr. John Fox had strong ambitions for Punahou's growth and excellence. He was fiercely competitive and wanted Punahou to be first among independent schools in both academics and athletics. Fox and Punahou's principals left me full discretion in my approach to foreign language teaching and the development of foreign language offerings.

When I arrived at Punahou in 1951, foreign language course options were meager: just a two-year sequence of French and two years of Latin, in addition to the beginning of German instruction. Within a few years of my arrival I was given the responsibility of chairing the foreign language department. I faced great challenges: the expansion of foreign language offerings, giving more choices to students; introducing Asian languages, particularly Japanese and Chinese; increasing the depth of foreign language teaching by lengthening the language teaching sequence to achieve a higher degree of competence; the improvement of teaching methods, bringing language learning to life as a tool for communication and as a vehicle for cultural understanding; and, most importantly, bringing excellent language teachers to Punahou, teachers who would set high standards and stimulate our students. Over the years I was able to make significant strides in meeting all these challenges.

In my approach to the spirit and methodology of teaching foreign languages, I stressed authenticity in transmitting the culture of another country, bringing the language alive through direct communication, introducing the spoken

The author teaching French at Punahou. Student exercises are on the blackboard.

language from the very beginning of instruction, and making language learning an enjoyable experience. I encouraged the use of audiovisual aids, such as tapes and films, invited visitors from other countries to speak to the students, and laid the groundwork of what was later to become an active and vibrant study exchange program with schools in the Asia-Pacific region and Europe.

I felt strongly that foreign language teachers, to be effective, had to be authentic models in the transmission of culture, preferably native speakers of the target language. It was a worthy aim but caused me occasional problems as department chair. Some of the European and Asian teachers I brought to Punahou, often new to Hawai'i and to the United States, experienced difficulties in relating to American adolescents and to the American school atmosphere. In most cases they learned to cope and win the respect and even affection of their students.

Punahou's boarding department, soon to be phased out, was still in operation when I came to the school. I recall spending many an evening helping dorm students with tutorials and homework. Punahou claimed my total commitment of time and effort, which consisted of preparing lesson plans and teaching, reading papers and tests, attending meetings,

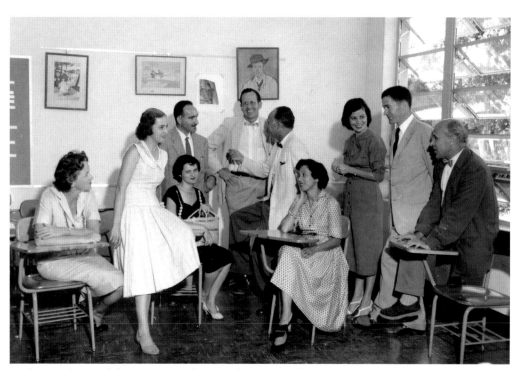

With members of the Punahou foreign language department in 1965.

conducting conferences with students, and acting as adviser to students in their extracurricular activities.

As the foreign language curriculum added length and depth to instruction, my teaching load included offering surveys of German and French literature, preparing my students for advanced college placement. For me as their teacher and for my students in advanced classes, this required intensive reading of novels and poetry and the preparation for the discussion of the literary selections in German or French. Often these readings came to me as my first contact with a given literary masterpiece. Reading ahead of my students, I learned through teaching! I enjoyed these classes immensely and hoped that I transmitted this enjoyment to my students.

With my family in 1962. This image is a composite of three photos and includes Malia twice, being held by both parents. Left to right: I am holding Malia, David, Dita, Larry, and Pi'ilani holding Malia.

These Punahou commitments placed strains on my marriage. On many evenings, when Pi'ilani wanted to go out to a movie or visit friends, I would be too busy reading student papers or preparing lesson plans. I recall her saying to me in exasperation: "Are you married to me or to Punahou?" I realized then that I had to find a balance between professional duties and family life. My solution was to wake up as early as three or four o'clock in the morning to work on my classes, allowing me to devote evenings to Pi'ilani and the family.

FAMILY AND COMMUNITY IN HAWAI'I

Our family life soon changed with the arrival in 1951 of our first son, David, followed in rapid succession by daughter Dita, a second son Larry, and later, in 1961, by our second daughter Malia. Spending their childhood and early school years in faculty residences on the Punahou School campus, each of the children developed unique personalities, identifying strongly with their Hawaiian heritage.

Living on campus, our children soon became part of a group of faculty children who enjoyed the benefits of large playing fields and a swimming pool. They formed close friendships at Punahou, which continue to the present. To be sure, they felt some pressures as faculty children, with expectations for good behavior and academic performance. Larry, in particular, given his learning handicaps, would have benefited from a more relaxed school environment with less pressure. During vacation times and in the summers, we would often take the children to the Big Island, where they stayed with their Hawaiian grandparents in Hilo. Reflecting the culture of the 1960s, David and Dita were drawn to the rural lifestyle of the Big Island, away from the hustle and urban tempo of Honolulu.

Looking back to the time when the children were growing up on the Punahou campus, I reflect on my various roles as husband, father, and teacher. My professional obligations at Punahou and my community involvement often took precedence over my family commitments, creating occasional tensions at home. Pi'ilani tended to be temperamental in dealing with the children, feeling often that I was not giving her sufficient support in parenting and in managing home life. These tensions increased as the children became teenagers during the rebellious atmosphere of the 1960s. Our youngest daughter, Malia, born in 1961, had a much calmer childhood than her older siblings, thriving at Punahou and in her later academic career.

After graduation from Punahou, David, adopting the Hawaiian first name of Kawika, established himself on the Big Island, where he raised his family and became a builder and general contractor. Dita also moved to the Big Island, where she completed her undergraduate studies at the University of Hawai'i's Hilo campus. Deeply Hawaiian in spirit and disposition, she related strongly to her grandparents, as well as to a circle of Punahou friends, several of whom had settled

David holding the August 21, 1959 *Honolulu Star-Bulletin*.

on the Big Island. Attracted to literature and to a career in education, Dita returned to Honolulu, earned a graduate degree in library science, and found her vocation as librarian at Punahou School. Dita built a house on a plot of land next to my home in the Maunawili valley on the windward side of O'ahu, where she established her family life and raised her two children.

Larry, our second son, struggled with medical problems that began in his early teens, causing a severe attention deficit and difficulties in focusing on his school tasks. These problems, though now stabilized with medication, continue to affect his adult life. Despite these obstacles, he has managed to cope bravely, leading a quiet married life and working on a farm on rural O'ahu.

Malia, our youngest child, continued her university studies on the U.S. mainland after graduating from Punahou.

She received her undergraduate and two graduate degrees at the University of California Berkeley, specializing in social work and public health. Her career in California has focused on early childhood issues, working on health education and child care policy. With her husband, a member of the Berkeley faculty, and two daughters, Malia leads an active professional and family life in California.

While our children were small and Pi'ilani continued her employment at Pearl Harbor, we had live-in help for support with household duties. One girl, Darlene Keju, hailing from the Marshall Islands of Micronesia, was to live with us for many years, becoming a virtual member of our family and a sister to our children.

After Darlene received her graduate degree in public health, she returned to Micronesia and became a youth leader and anti-nuclear activist, advocating a nuclear-free Pacific.

With Darlene Keju from Ebeye island.

Chatting with France's most famous entertainer, Maurice Chevalier, during his visit to the Punahou campus as part of an Alliance Française program, established to help the French language come alive for students. An aide carries the straw hats which Chevalier traditionally wore when he performed.

Tragically, she died prematurely of breast cancer, probably as a result of lingering radiation from atomic testing at the Eniwetok and Bikini atolls.

Stimulated by Pi'ilani's vivacious and welcoming personality, we enjoyed an active social life and opened our campus home to many visitors and dinner parties, a boon to our marriage. In addition to family circles, we both had many friends in the wider Honolulu community, which featured a growing cultural life, such as the symphony and the Academy of Arts. Hawai'i became a state in 1959. Some of our Hawaiian friends, including Pi'ilani, had mixed feelings about statehood for Hawai'i, changing the life style on the islands, expanding commerce, and causing some alienation. As a transplanted European, I welcomed statehood and its benefits from representation in Congress. I felt that the Hawaiian spirit could be maintained, even as we became the 50th state of the union.

Hawai'i Chapter - American Red Cross

First Lady Eleanor Roosevelt during a 1943 wartime trip to the Pacific theatre.

MRS. FRANKLIN D. ROOSEVELT
211 EAST 62ND STREET
NEW YORK 21, N. Y.

April 4, 1957

Dear Mr. Ramler:

Thank you so much for your kind invitation which I appreciate.

Unfortunately, I cannot go to Hawaii while I am on the West Coast this month. I might consider going to you next autumn *In water* if I can find some friends who would care to join me.

With many regrets,

Very sincerely yours,

Eleanor Roosevelt

I invited former First Lady Eleanor Roosevelt to Hawai'i to meet community groups and students.

INTERNATIONAL OUTREACH AT PUNAHOU

In my teaching and in my relations with students, I was committed from the beginning at Punahou to link the classroom experience to the community outside the school—locally, nationally, and internationally. As a teacher of French, I felt strongly that the study of French language and culture should find an echo in the community and provide relevance and stimulation to the students. In cooperation with friends and community members interested in French culture, this aim led me to found a Hawai'i branch of the Paris-based Alliance Française. Under the sponsorship of the Alliance, we were able to bring French classical theater to Honolulu, presenting high quality performances for students and the community at large. In addition, we offered French lectures and recitals, and provided summer scholarships to teachers of French language for study at French universities.

We sponsored such diverse speakers as the philosopher Gabriel Marcel and the entertainer Maurice Chevalier. In Honolulu for a one-man show, Chevalier made a memorable appearance at Punahou's Dillingham Hall, lured to the stage by a bevy of attractive multiethnic Punahou girls. Monsieur Robert Luc, Consul General of France in San Francisco at the time, was of great help to me in these endeavors and became a good friend. Key Honolulu donors in support of the Alliance Française were francophile Frank Hecht, who served as the first president, and his wife Anita, who continued to be active after Frank passed away.

My extracurricular activities at Punahou included advising the Forum and Debate Club, assisting Punahou's early participation in the Pacific and Asian Affairs Council's high school program, and advising the Model United Nations program. These activities attracted outstanding students,

for me a source of great satisfaction. One special experience stands out. In cooperation with the Pacific and Asian Affairs Council, *The Honolulu Advertiser*, the morning newspaper, announced a statewide research contest open to all Island schools, focusing on a critical issue in foreign relations.

The Punahou team's topic was "The Foreign Policy of Red China as Seen through Chinese Eyes." ("Red China" was still a term used at that time). I advised the team of five students who worked with remarkable diligence, searching for primary sources and treating the topic thoroughly from various perspectives. The students spent many weekends on the research project at our home, with Pi'ilani typing various drafts. The Punahou team—Brian Lederer, Galen Fox, John Goodbody, Robert Yoshioka, and Stuart Kiang—was rewarded by receiving the first prize in the State of Hawai'i, with an invitation to be hosted by Hawai'i's congressional delegation in Washington and by the UN headquarters in New York.

In Washington we met Vice President Lyndon Johnson, Speaker of the House Sam Rayburn, and Senator Thomas Dodd of Connecticut, whom I had known in Nuremberg when he served as deputy to Justice Robert Jackson. A particular honor for the group was the introduction of the research paper into the Congressional Record by Hawai'i's Senator Oren E. Long. In a session at the State Department, the chief of the China desk took time to discuss the paper with the students. The unique honor of having their paper taken seriously by a policy maker proved more significant and transforming than any other experience in Washington. One student, Galen Fox, later joined the State Department as foreign service officer in Taiwan and Hong Kong.

The Punahou Forum Club, again in cooperation with

Punahou students with members of Hawai'i's Congressional delegation in April 1961. Left to right: the author, Galen Fox, Stuart Kiang, Senator Hiram Fong, Robert Yoshioka, Senator Oren E. Long, Brian Lederer, Rep. Daniel Inouye, and John Goodbody.

The Honolulu Advertiser, presented a series of panel forums, where key Hawai'i leaders from state and city government, the legislature, and industry would appear before the senior student body and answer questions posed by a panel of students. These sessions would be recorded, transcribed, and edited, and would appear in the Sunday *Advertiser*.

In the 1950s I served as President of the Hawai'i Branch of the United Nations Association of the United States. This service coincided with Japan's admission in 1956 to the United Nations and stimulated our branch to organize a community wide celebration. This task brought me into first contact with the Japanese consulate in Honolulu, in particular with Consul General Masahide Kanayama, who was later to become Japan's Ambassador to Korea. We had a most successful event with cultural presentations and the participation of five hundred celebrants at the Hilton Hawaiian Village's Long House. Congratulatory messages included a warm note from Eleanor Roosevelt.

Open summers and sabbatical leaves are an invaluable bonus of an academic career. Over the years I took advantage of many opportunities for travel and enrichment. In the summer of 1958 I enrolled in an international gathering in Paris under the sponsorship of the University of Paris, the Sorbonne, entitled "Rencontre Internationale" (International Encounter), bringing together French-speaking young leaders from various professions and from various countries for lectures, briefings, and joint activities. Interestingly, my current affiliation, Hawai'i's East-West Center, offers a similar program every year with focus on the Asia-Pacific region. I decided to reach Paris on a round-the-world air ticket with stops in Tokyo, Hong Kong, and Bangkok. At all these brief stops I made contact with United Nations Association representatives and enjoyed warm hospitality.

In Tokyo I stayed at Frank Lloyd Wright's original Imperial Hotel, since then razed and replaced. In 1958 Japan had not yet fully recovered from the war and still showed traces of third world conditions. In Hong Kong I stayed with a cousin at his house on the peak overlooking Hong Kong Harbor. After completion of his medical studies, he settled in Hong Kong from Europe and joined a British doctor's practice. Interned by the Japanese during the war, he was released to ease the wartime shortage of doctors in Hong Kong. He became senior physician in a busy medical practice, mostly serving Europeans and international diplomatic personnel. I saw him again in Hong Kong, London, and at his later home in Vancouver, where he passed away several years ago.

Local Japanese language newspaper, *Hawaii Hochi*, covered the celebration of Japan's admission to the United Nations at the Hawaiian Village. Pi'ilani and I are at left, with dignitaries including Consul General Masahide Kanayama and his wife in center.

SABBATICAL LEAVE IN THE SOUTH OF FRANCE

I took advantage of Punahou's generous sabbatical leave policy by spending a full semester and summer in the south of France, settling in the beautiful Roman city of Aix-en-Provence, seat of a fine university and an artistic center in Provence. We traveled to Europe *en famille* with our four children and also with Pi'ilani's parents, who stayed with us for the duration of the sabbatical. To accommodate our large family, we took delivery of a Volkswagen van in Munich, attended the wedding of Pi'ilani's younger brother, stationed in Munich with the U.S. Army, and drove via Paris to Provence. Along the hilly outskirts of Aix-en-Provence, an area famous for Cezanne's Mont Saint Victoire paintings, we were fortunate to find a large furnished villa for rent, just perfect for our family.

We enrolled the three older children in French schools, and I registered for courses at the University of Aix Marseille.

On sabbatical in France. L-R: Annie Ahuna, Larry, me, Moses Ahuna, David, Pi'ilani, Malia, and Dita.

The children adapted very quickly to their new surroundings. Within a short time they managed to communicate in French and brought classmates home to play. On weekends we went on long drives around the Provence region, and during school holidays we traveled to Spain or Italy. It was an idyllic time and a great opportunity for the entire family. My father-in-law, anxious to keep busy during our stay in France, wanted to cultivate some of the land around the villa and grow vegetables. When we asked the owner's agent for permission to dig up some earth, we were told that nothing could grow in that area, but we were welcome to try. So the Hawaiian visitor connected an irrigation system, toiled the land, purchased seeds for planting, and, sure enough, within a few weeks the first crops sprouted! The news spread and neighbors came by to admire the work of the Hawaiian farmer, a miracle worker who made the arid area bloom.

In France I gathered resources to support Punahou's French language program. I traveled frequently to Paris to select teaching materials, such as realia, tapes, and slides, as well as up-to-date teaching methodology.

Soon after return to Hawai'i and Punahou I was again faced with a decision with consequences for my career and for our family. The headmaster of Iolani School, an outstanding independent school in Hawai'i, had accepted a position in Europe as president of the American School of Paris. He approached me with an offer to go with him to Paris as principal of the American School under generous conditions and with good salary. Though going to Paris would uproot our family, Pi'ilani, always the adventurer, was open to the idea and left the decision up to me. While tempted by this interesting offer, I turned it down. However stimulating the job in Paris might be, the American School of Paris served a transient student population and attracted a transient faculty.

As a foreign school, operating in France on the periphery rather than the mainstream of education, it had limited impact. Punahou, on the other hand, was deeply rooted in the community and ranked among the top independent schools in the United States.

A NEW POSITION AT PUNAHOU

Dr. Rod McPhee, who had replaced John Fox as Punahou's president, made me another proposal, which clinched my decision to remain at Punahou. He offered me a new position as Director of Instructional Services and Coordinator of Curriculum, with responsibilities spanning the entire school, both the elementary and secondary divisions. The task was to coordinate and consolidate the school's support services, including its three libraries and its growing technical infrastructure, articulate the curricular offerings from K-12, and administer professional development programs for the faculty. For me it was time for a change, and I accepted this challenge with enthusiasm.

To bring fresh ideas and innovations to Punahou, I joined the network of the Association for Supervision and Curriculum Development, based in Alexandria, Virginia, which held conferences throughout the United States. In later years I was to chair the international outreach of this national association, expanding its programs and publications. This affiliation brought me into contact with stimulating educators throughout the country, allowing me to bring many of them to Punahou for presentations and workshops for our faculty. It was also an opportunity for Punahou to reach out to other schools, both private and public, and include them in our professional development.

I felt strongly that Punahou, although independent in its governance, should not isolate itself behind the walls

As Punahou's Director of Instructional Services and Coordinator of Curriculum.

and hedges surrounding the eighty acres of the campus, but should commit itself to its public purpose and responsibility, both in Hawai'i and beyond. Hawai'i's island community, with its Polynesian roots and its strong Asian identity, with immigrant populations from China, Japan, Korea, the Philippines, and Pacific islands, gave us an opportunity and an obligation to reflect our multiethnic heritage through educational outreach. This outward look, fortunately shared by many colleagues, trustees, and administrators, led to initiatives that were to define much of my career at Punahou.

INTERNATIONAL OUTREACH

My first international outreach attempt was directed at Tahiti, our Polynesian cousin south of the equator. Establishing contacts with Tahiti offered multiple gains: strengthening our common Polynesian roots, and benefiting our language department through the proximity of a French-speaking community. When I first went to Tahiti in the 1960s, both in my Punahou School capacity and as president of the Alliance Française of Hawai'i, I was welcomed with open arms. In Pape'ete I met with leading educators and government officials, all enthusiastic about launching a student exchange and cooperating in educational programs.

Among the government officials was Gaston Flosse, mayor of Pirae, a suburb of Pape'ete, who was later to become President of French Polynesia. For me this was the first of many visits to French Polynesia, where I count many friends and collaborators. On that first trip I recall being met at the airport by Tahiti's director of tourism, Alec Ata, later to become foreign minister, who was my host and guide to all the islands of the Society chain.

Despite all the good will, at first we found it very difficult to launch an educational exchange program between Hawaiian and Tahitian schools. We lacked a structural and financial framework that could support an exchange of students. Furthermore, Punahou's charter at the time did not provide for liability for foreign students, such as housing with host families and extracurricular activities beyond the campus and school hours. To launch international programs at Punahou with the necessary responsibility and oversight, we established the Foundation for Study in Hawai'i and Abroad, with its seat at Punahou under my directorship, but fiscally and structurally independent of Punahou. Creating this foundation would also provide the possibility of participation

and financial support to deserving non-Punahou students applying from the Hawai'i community at large.

The first chairman of the new foundation's board was a close friend, Frank Damon, member of an old-line Hawai'i family, an attorney and also a Punahou trustee, who shared my commitment to international education. Punahou's president and several other members of the school's Board of Trustees also joined the foundation, assuring a solid support for launching international programs. My office at Punahou carried out the dual functions of school-wide instructional services and the foundation's administration.

Outreach to Japan was a high priority. Hawai'i has close ties to Japan through its large Japanese ethnic population and through its major role as a destination for tourists from Japan. With Japan's rapid economic growth and its impact on Asia and the world came a strong interest in cultural contacts and study programs. We had introduced Japanese language instruction at Punahou, which soon overtook European languages in the students' choices. I was convinced that establishing contacts with Japan would strengthen the Japanese curriculum and provide enrichment to our students.

THE KEIO JAPAN CONNECTION

At that time a fortuitous encounter was to have a far-reaching impact on Punahou's future relationships with Japan. At a dinner given at the University of Hawai'i, I was seated next to a visiting Japanese educator from Tokyo's distinguished Keio University, Professor Eiichi Kiyoka, who at the time was director of Keio's International House. Having studied at Cornell, he spoke fluent English and was the author of an English language textbook. One of his previous positions was as principal of Yoshisha, Keio's well known elementary school. Beyond his academic background,

With Professor Eiichi Kiyoka of Keio University.

Kiyoka-Sensei carried a special personal pedigree as great-grandson of Fukuzawa Yukichi, leading figure of the Meiji era, founder of Keio University, and who still appears today on Japan's ten thousand Yen bank note.

Kiyoka-Sensei was the translator into English of Fukuzawa's autobiography and his many other writings. Fukuzawa holds credit for opening Japan to Western ideas and culture during the Meiji era and for influencing the international stance of Keio, the university he founded. The dinner conversation with Kiyoka-Sensei led me to invite him to Punahou, where he was impressed not only by its current role and offerings, but also by its history and its founding in the 19th century, along a timeline similar to that of Keio.

Kiyoka-Sensei and I found that we had much in common. At a dinner at my home, I broached the idea of educational exchanges between Keio's high schools and Punahou. He immediately welcomed this initiative and promised to follow through upon his return to Japan. Thus began a close relationship between Keio and Punahou, which continues strongly.

For me the personal contact with Kiyoka-Sensei illustrated a key factor governing relationships with Asian counterparts. The importance of face-to-face meetings, along with social contacts and the development of friendships, cannot be overestimated. Before meeting Kiyoka-Sensei, I had written to several academic institutions in Japan exploring educational exchanges, but received no response. I realized that without a personal contact or at least a go-between, there was no impetus for a Japanese institution to react, especially when the inquiry came from a foreign country.

LAUNCHING THE PAN PACIFIC PROGRAM

My meeting with Kiyoka-Sensei yielded quick results. In the summer of 1969, we welcomed the first group of Keio students to Punahou for a four-week session of English instruction and Hawai'i exploration. I recall that first group of Keio students arriving at the Honolulu airport, dressed formally in coats and ties, looking serious and apprehensive, as if they were carrying the weight of Japan on their shoulders. Soon, however, the warmth and hospitality of their host families dissipated their weariness. Four weeks later, at their departure, the scene at the airport was totally different. Clad in aloha shirts, bedecked with flower leis, the Keio students were sent off with hugs and tears.

We designated this session as the Pan Pacific Program, which has since grown and expanded to many other regions of Asia and the Pacific. The relationship with Keio continues with program alumni in Japan treasuring their study period in Hawai'i and their life with host parents. Naoyuki Agawa, a 1971 alumnus of the Punahou Pan Pacific program who has

First group of Keio students are welcomed at Punahou in 1969. Professor Kiyoka is at center front row flanked by Frank Damon and the author.

become a Japanese diplomat and law school professor, recalls his Hawai'i experience:

> "I need not tell you how much the summer of 1971 has meant to me. I made some of my best friends through the program. I met some wonderful people in Hawai'i that summer, including my host families, with whom I still keep in touch. Had I not participated in the program, I would not have gone to a U.S. college and a U.S. law school. I would not have started writing about America, and I would not have found myself in Charlottesville at the University of Virginia thinking about the United States Constitution and America's past and future."

Once the contact with Keio was established, it was feasible to bring Tahiti aboard, and we soon included Tahitian students in the Pan Pacific program. They added a welcome Polynesian presence to the mix of students. Over the years more regions and schools in Japan were added to the program, including the Katoh Schools of Numazu, the Tamagawa Schools on the outskirts of Tokyo, and the Nanzan school in Nagoya. Beyond Japan, the Pan Pacific program now includes students from China and several South-East Asia nations.

From the very beginning of the Pan Pacific Program, host families in Hawai'i have been its central feature. With traditional Hawaiian hospitality, Honolulu host parents have welcomed students from Asia and the Pacific into their homes where they joined family activities and experienced a slice of Hawaiian and American life. This family experience represents the heart of the program, leaves an indelible impression, and often marks the beginning of a lifelong relationship.

In addition to the Hawai'i-bound Pan Pacific Program, we initiated outbound programs beginning with destinations in Japan and Tahiti, and expanded later to other regions in Asia and Europe. As in Hawai'i, outbound programs, in addition to language and culture studies, also feature home stay with lasting impact.

For so many of the participating students, both from Hawai'i and from the Asia- Pacific region, these summer programs had a transforming impact, opening new horizons and influencing their further studies and choice of career. I continue to stay in contact with many Pan Pacific alumni. Their stories of personal and professional growth and impact remain a source of great satisfaction.

Advertiser Photo by Roy Ito

strange, new world of aloha

Come, come, it can't be that bad. Mrs. Allan Renton tries to present a lei to student Kenji Tachikawa, who obviously isn't used to the sometimes overwhelming charm of Hawaii. But after he's been here six weeks as part of the student group studying at Punahou, doubtless he will catch on. Story on Page A-2.

OPENING A CONTACT WITH CHINA

After President Richard Nixon and Secretary of State Henry Kissinger initiated contact with the People's Republic of China following decades of isolation, I saw the potential of offering our students the opportunity for a study experience in China. I started to write letters of inquiry to the foreign ministry in Beijing and later to the office of tourism, but received no reply.

Undaunted, I continued sending letters to Beijing until finally, in 1977, I received a one-sentence reply from the office of tourism: "Please send us some information about Punahou School and the Foundation for Study in Hawai'i and Abroad." Immediately I sent out brochures, including a statement of intent for the China visit, and received an invitation to visit China in the summer of 1978, one year before diplomatic relations were opened. To my knowledge, our visit to China that summer represented a breakthrough: the first school visit from the United States since the pre-Mao era. This visit included a group of students, accompanied by several parents, trustees, and Punahou's president.

Though we asked for an academic structure of the China experience, including a mix of study and travel, the first China programs, conducted by the Chinese national tourist office, offered basically a sightseeing tour to various destinations in the PRC. However, once in China we succeeded in establishing a relationship with the Beijing Teachers College, now renamed Capital Normal University. They offered us a study program of Chinese language at their campus, followed by travel with teaching staff to cultural destinations in China. I made these arrangements with that college's Dean of Chinese Studies, Wang Muzeng, who was to become

With Pan Pacific program students from Asia on a Big Island beach in 1995.

one of my closest friends in China, a friendship extending to his family and to the present time. At our invitation Dean Wang's son Ran, a gifted student, attended the Pan Pacific Program at Punahou, stayed on for his senior year to graduate from Punahou, received admission to Harvard, where he earned B.A. and M.B.A. degrees with honors, and now has become chief executive officer of a successful international financial services and brokerage firm in Beijing.

In a way this young man's story illustrates the remarkable and rapid transformation of China since its opening to the world in the late 1970s. For me it also illustrates the potential of education to affect lives and transform society.

Punahou's ties with Japanese and Chinese educational institutions grew over the years, along with expansion to other areas of the world. Outbound and inbound international programs expanded, with Punahou conducting workshops and hosting visits by educators and student groups from abroad.

CONTACTS WITH JAPAN

Links to Japan led to my participation in the founding of the Japan-America Society of Hawai'i, which aimed to increase understanding of Japanese cultural, social, and governmental developments. In my capacity as program chairman for the Society in its early years, followed by a term as its president from 1986 to 1987, I helped with initial contacts in Japan, bringing speakers from various Japanese governmental and cultural sectors to the Hawaiian community. One of the early personalities whom I invited to speak in Honolulu—he later became a part-time Hawai'i resident—was the late Akio Morita, co-founder and chairman of the Sony Corporation. Mr. Morita was a great supporter of international education, contributing to Punahou's technological expansion with a substantial range of support, including language laboratories and audiovisual equipment.

AUDIENCE WITH JAPAN'S EMPEROR AND EMPRESS

A special Japan-Hawai'i connection, with which I am closely involved as one of the founding trustees, springs from a gift by Japan's imperial family when the emperor and empress, at the time still Crown Prince and Crown Princess, visited Hawai'i in the 1960s. This visit launched a foundation, supported financially by Hawai'i and Japan, that sponsors scholarship grants awarded to selected graduate students at the University of Hawai'i to conduct academic research in Japan and, reciprocally, to Japanese students to conduct academic projects in Hawai'i.

A special bonus, connected with this scholarship grant, extends an invitation to an audience with the imperial couple at the palace, offered yearly to the selected students—two from Japan and two from Hawai'i—and to a Foundation trustee who can be in Japan at that time. Fortunate to benefit from this opportunity, I recall vividly the occasion in Tokyo when a black limousine carried us through the palace gate along tree-lined spacious grounds to the residence building, a low level modern structure with the classic lines of Japanese architecture. In a formal reception room we were met by the Grand Chamberlain, the Lady-in-Waiting, and an imperial household official who briefed us on seating arrangements and procedures in the audience room. The Emperor and Empress greeted us at the room's entrance with warm smiles and handshakes, took their seats on a settee in front of an open window facing the garden, and began an informal conversation with questions directed at the students about their projects and plans.

An interpreter from the Ministry of Foreign Affairs placed herself behind me and whispered a translation of the conversation. I was impressed by the benign face of the

Audience with Emperor Akihito and Empress Michiko in June, 2002 at the Tokyo imperial residence. Two American and two Japanese recipients of the Akihito Scholarship grant face the imperial couple. Left to right: John Treiber, Scott Mudd, Rino Kawase, Aya Kitamura, the author, an interpreter, fellow trustee Jean Rolles and Yoshio Nakamura, Director General of Keidanren, the Japanese partner institution for the administration of the scholarship.

empress, her beatific smile, and her elegant bearing, matched by the emperor's kind and earnest questioning and interest. As the audience ended, the emperor and empress shook hands again with all of us as we left the room. By extending their hand, the emperor and empress relieved the foreign visitor from executing a proper bow—a graceful gesture! One of the Japanese students at the audience, filled with emotion, said to me as we walked down the corridor: "Am I dreaming or is this really happening to me?" We then boarded a minibus for a special tour of the inner gardens, rarely open to visitors. Unlike the palace grounds of Versailles ouside Paris, where the trees and shrubs are clipped and shaped, here the trees grow naturally, allowing a flow of vistas with mounds, rocks, and a variety of flowers and plants. To me it evoked an impressionist landscape, as depicted by Monet's paintings of Giverny.

ESTABLISHING THE WO INTERNATIONAL CENTER

Speaking at the Wo Center dedication.

Increasing international activity brought out the need for a physical base and a center for the school's international programs and initiatives. Here we were beneficiaries of generous gifts by two influential Hawai'i merchant and banking families with strong ties to Punahou. The C.S. Wo family and the K.J. Luke family made it possible to establish and build the Wo International Center. These two families, whose children and grandchildren are Punahou alumni, and with business links to Asia and Europe, recognized the importance of international study experiences for Punahou students and for the Hawai'i community. As they expressed their interest in helping to build a center, I realized the importance of establishing firm roots for our international programs which would last and grow beyond my tenure, something to express Punahou's enduring commitment to international education. The Wo International Center absorbed the previous Foundation for Study in Hawai'i and Abroad and became an integral and vital part of Punahou School's international functions.

Centrally located on the campus, a handsome building was erected with an auditorium, classroom, and office spaces, including administrative and technological support for the center's functions. A noted artist and art collector, the late John Young, donated outstanding art objects and paintings from Asia, the Pacific, and other parts of the world to decorate the center's entrance lobbies and walls, creating a mini-museum for students participating in the center's classes and activities. The Wo Center's physical and programmatic presence on campus, unique in the United States, represents living testimony to the ongoing commitment of Punahou to its outreach to the world. For me, responsibilities at the center required frequent travel abroad to discuss and launch joint programs and activities, taking me to partner institutions in many parts of the world, but most often to Japan and China. Contacts with China evolved and increased with support of Beijing's Soong Ching Ling Foundation, opening contacts with key educational institutions in China. The aims of this educational and cultural Chinese foundation, established in memory of Soong Ching Ling, spouse of the historical figure Sun Yat-Sen, relate closely to Punahou's outreach to China. Our interests in developing educational opportunities for Hawai'i's students coincided with a reciprocal and growing response by schools in the Asia-Pacific region to build international bridges for language study and cultural understanding. The resulting partnerships and friendships have become a significant source of satisfaction to me, both professionally and personally. After my retirement from Punahou School in 1995, the Wo International Center continued and expanded its functions with a dedicated and effective staff.

Left-Right: Jim Wo, Kan Jan Luke, Punahou president Dr. Roderick McPhee, me, and Bob Wo at the Wo International Center dedication in May 1993. The Wo and Luke families were the Center's key benefactors.

International partners gather at the dedication of the Wo International Center in1993. Left to right: The author, Miss Toyoko Naganuma (Japan, Keio), Dr. Masahide Katoh and John Maher (Japan, Numazu), Robert Koenig (Tahiti), Professor Eiichi Kiyoka and Mrs. Ebihara (Japan, Keio), Professor Wang Zhen Tang (China), Natasha Proskurina (Russia).

PI'ILANI'S ILLNESS: THE ALZHEIMER SYNDROME

My professional life in Hawai'i, as well as my community activities involved frequent travel abroad. As a devoted and lively companion and as a warm hostess, Pi'ilani supported me while also volunteering on behalf of Hawai'i cultural offerings and charities, such as the ballet and the heart association. Tragically, in the fall of 1978, she was diagnosed by a neurologist as suffering from Alzheimer's syndrome. A series of incidents revealed memory loss, pronunciation errors, and deficiency in comprehension and speech. She became subject to mood swings, ranging from euphoria to almost uncontrollable anger and depression. As a husband, I was confronted with challenges on a daily basis. Our relationship changed from two individuals with compatible intellectual and emotional reactions to roles as caregiver and patient. When care and love are extended, and a positive and comfortable environment is created, I believe that the Alzheimer patient can be happy for a substantial part of the time. In a family relationship this situation calls for an attempt to reach a kind of love which the Greeks call *agape*, which is essentially selfless and in which one cannot expect the normal ranges of reciprocity.

Piilani's condition deteriorated rapidly and we could no longer keep her at home. She spent nineteen years under good care in a nursing home on the Big Island, until she passed away in 2003.

Pi'ilani found peace and drew her last breath at the Hilo Life Care Center, where she had been a resident patient since 1984, most of that time unable to communicate or relate to her surroundings. The Lani I knew as a warm and dynamic spirit really left us in 1978. For most of twenty-five years, although her body continued to function, she lived a life isolated from family and friends in the dark fog of her illness. However, all who knew her cherish the memory of her vibrant personality and her many contributions, which touched us during her active years in Hawai'i from the 1950s to the 1970s. With her background as a court reporter at the Nuremberg trials, travels and residence in Europe, and a wide range of interests, Pi'ilani

was a cosmopolitan Hawaiian woman who made a strong and unforgettable impact on all who crossed her path, both socially and professionally.

As my wife, she was the catalyst for my life and career in Hawai'i; as a mother, she reared four fine children; and as a friend, she enriched us all.

My life alone during the years of Pi'ilani's stay at the nursing home and after her passing resulted in more of my time devoted to professional and community activities, as well as to frequent travel. I was able to give a portion of the land surrounding my Maunawili home on the windward side of O'ahu to my daughter Dita and her family, which enabled her to build a house next to mine. This proximity strengthened family bonds, creating a Ramler compound, contributing to a quality of life which I continue to enjoy to this day. Especially I welcome the opportunity of gatherings at our home with the Ramler extended family, including grandchildren who seem to appreciate and enjoy the link with grandpa.

INTERNATIONAL TRAVEL, WRITING, & LECTURING

My stay in Paris in the summer of 1968 coincided with student strikes and massive street demonstrations protesting educational policies of the DeGaulle government (and eventually leading to its collapse). Students occupied the Left Bank, holding sit-ins and bringing commerce and traffic to a halt. Among the student demonstrators were several girls from Hawai'i who had been my students at Punahou. My articles on these incidents appeared in *The Honolulu Advertiser* and came as a shock to their parents!

An invitation by the German foreign ministry in the 1980s to visit several German cities to explore educational policy and programs resulted in another series of articles for the Honolulu morning newspaper.

A summer Fulbright grant to Israel in 1981, based at Jerusalem's Hebrew University, enabled me to explore the country intensively through a combination of lectures, field trips, and discussions. This experience led to a follow-up visit and a magazine article on Arab-Israeli issues entitled "Schools for Peace." A special bonus of the Fulbright grant to Israel was the opportunity to visit my two sisters and their families.

An exploratory trip to Russia took me to the city of Magadan in Siberia, which was the administrative center of the Gulag prison camps during the Stalin era. In Magadan I was a house guest in the home of a school principal and was warmly entertained by Russian families.

Visiting with my sisters Lotte and Adele, in Israel.

115

JOINING THE EAST-WEST CENTER

After my long tenure of forty-four years at Punahou ended with retirement in 1995, I faced the challenge of structuring my future, particularly of continuing my efforts in international education. To enable me to be professionally active and effective, I needed an institutional base, an environment and a stimulation in which I could join with individuals committed to similar goals. An invitation from Hawai'i's East-West Center to come aboard as a volunteer fellow in its educational program was very welcome. At that time the Center was going through a transition with new leadership, new priorities and a review of its programs. My long experience at Punahou in coordinating curriculum, in launching a foundation for international studies, and in establishing structures and programs for the Wo International Center could be applied to challenges at the East-West Center. For me it was a natural sequel to my international efforts at Punahou, and also an appropriate time to move into a new environment with new dimensions and relationships. At the East-West Center I especially enjoyed collegial and stimulating relationships with researchers and members of the staff, collaborating on a variety of educational projects.

One of my early initiatives at the Center focused on elementary and secondary teachers of Hawaiian language and Polynesian culture. Building on my previous contacts with French Polynesia, I organized a study experience in Tahiti under the title "Linking Cousins of the Pacific." The consultant for this venture was Dr. Yosihiko Sinoto, the noted archeologist of

Her "crab-claw" sails filled with wind, the voyaging canoe *Hokule'a* is on a practice run before her first historic sail to Tahiti in 1976. The vessel has since voyaged throughout the Polynesian Triangle navigating traditionally without instruments using only natural signs. I was a founding member of the Polynesian Voyaging Society, which built, and still sails, the canoe.

Polynesia based at Hawai'i's Bishop Museum. The experience in Tahiti extended to an exploration of archeological sites and findings on several islands of the Society chain, and also included a survey of contemporary issues facing Tahiti through presentations and site visits on the main island of Tahiti.

Related to this effort to link Hawai'i and Tahiti was my involvement as a founding member of the board of directors of the Polynesian Voyaging Society, which built *Hokule'a*, a replica of the double-hulled canoes that were sailed across the Pacific by the early Polynesians. Since *Hokule'a*'s memorable first voyage in 1976, commemorating the U.S. bicentennial year, many more voyages across the Pacific have taken place, reinforcing the cultural bonds linking the Pacific islands.

Beijing: The opening of an educational program sponsored by the East-West Center in cooperation with China's Ministry of Education and Peking University: The Institute on Teaching About China and the United States.

Indeed, *Hokule'a* has recently completed a voyage to Japan, achieving a special and meaningful link.

A key program of the East-West Center's education group in which I collaborate as coordinator features a cooperative venture with China's Ministry of Education and Peking University. It brings Chinese scholars to the United States for a three-week program during which they travel to various parts of the country and explore issues pertaining to contemporary U.S. society and government. Reciprocally, in alternate years the program takes selected U.S. scholars to various parts of China for an authentic survey of aspects of China's development.

The preparation and conduct of this program bring me frequently to China, both in preparation of these programs and in their conduct in China and the United States. The contacts with educators in China represent a special bonus of this program, creating a network of personal and professional friendships. Starting with the Punahou programs at the end of the 1970s and extending to the East-West Center's programs

continuing to date, my China connection has placed me as a witness to the remarkable development and rise of China from the end of the cultural revolution to the nation's present position as a dynamic presence in Asia with global impact.

At the East-West Center I became involved with another initiative, launched under the title "New Paradigms for Education in the 21st Century" and later adapted to "International Forum for Education 2020." This program, with participation of scholars from the Asia-Pacific region, aims to explore and challenge education's function and impact in the rapidly changing environment of the 21st century. It is an ongoing effort, featuring publications, seminars, and institutes.

Spearheading this initiative, the East-West Center faces an important challenge in examining principles and criteria governing educational structures and practices. For me the intellectual stimulation and exchange of ideas has been most rewarding. While my East-West Center involvement now targets mainly post-secondary education, I continue

Beijing, 1993. With Wang Muzeng, Dean of Chinese Studies at Beijing's Capital Normal University.

ties to the elementary and secondary sectors, serving on the advisory board of the Wo International Center and as a trustee of Saint Francis School, a private Catholic school in Honolulu. The Saint Francis School connection has a personal aspect: Piilani's youngest sister, my sister-in-law, lives and serves at that school as a retired nun. In recognition of her long and devoted service to the Saint Francis community as leader and teacher, a newly constructed gymnasium carries her name.

THE PACIFIC BASIN CONSORTIUM

In cooperation with the Hawai'i Association of Independent Schools I was involved in launching an internationally collaborative initiative, the Pacific Basin Consortium. Targeting mainly independent schools in the Asia-Pacific region, the aim was to bring educators from various countries to a forum and create a network for educational exchange, learning from each other and cooperating in educational projects through international and regional conferences and workshops. Hawai'i was an appropriate cross-cultural bridge for this effort, serving as headquarters for the project and hosting several successful conferences. From 1995 to 2003, I served the consortium as its president, gaining greatly from the opportunity to interact with schools and teachers throughout the Asia-Pacific region. This initiative brought me into contact with the National Association of Independent Schools, based in Washington, D.C., which serves as a coordinating center for independent schools throughout the United States. The editor of the association's journal, *Independent School*, asked me to contribute to the international section of the journal and write a series of articles on cutting edge educational issues and developments in various countries. Capitalizing on my professional travel for Punahou School and the East-West Center, I focused my articles on contemporary educational issues in such countries as Japan, China, India, New Zealand, Israel, and the European Union. In addition to articles for publication, I also wrote essays on various travel destinations, which I sent to a network of friends and family. Professional exploration and journalistic tasks gave meaning to my experiences, adding context and color to contacts with people and places, stimulating me to preserve my experiences in articles and journals.

MEETING KIYOKO

One of my travels to Tahiti led to my meeting Kiyoko, the woman who was to become my companion and wife. As has happened so often in my life, that meeting was an example of serendipity, of an unplanned and fortuitous encounter.

TRAVELS WITH KIYOKO

In front of an Egyptian pyramid.

In Japan's Kansai region during cherry blossom season.

Visiting a glacier in Argentina.

Kiyoko strikes a yoga pose at Machu Picchu.

After preparation in Papeʻete for an East-West Center study program, I found myself with two free days before catching the weekly flight back to Honolulu. I decided to fly over to Bora Bora, a beautiful island in the Society chain, famed for swimming and snorkeling in its lagoon. After the Bora Bora interlude, while waiting for a ferry to take passengers to the Bora Bora airstrip for the flight back to Papeʻete, I smiled and said *konnichi-wa* to two Japanese ladies standing at the pier. This greeting led to the obligatory taking of photos and exchanging of visiting cards.

A few weeks later I received an envelope from Japan with the photos, announcing that Kiyoko would visit Hawaiʻi the following week. We met for dinner, conversed at length, starting a bond that eventually led to our marriage and life together in Hawaiʻi. Though Kiyoko's English was halting at the time, we communicated well and discovered that we had much in common. Kiyoko, then separated from her husband and later divorced, had experienced a tragedy which changed the course of her life. At the age of fourteen, her daughter, a bright and beautiful child, was diagnosed with leukemia, and had to spend a year under intensive care in a Kyoto hospital until she passed away. Kiyoko gave up her business to be near her daughter at the Kyoto hospital.

After her daughter's death and the separation from her husband, Kiyoko found it difficult to settle down and traveled frequently abroad in the company of lady friends. Her trip to Tahiti at that time led to our meeting. Piʻilani's long stay in a nursing home, and her eventual death, represented in some way a parallel to Kiyoko's experience, intensifying our bond.

After our initial meeting, Kiyoko visited me frequently in Hawaiʻi, often joining me on trips to various countries. As a Japanese national, she traveled to the United States under the visa waiver program that limited her stay to a maximum of three months, requiring frequent Japan-Hawaiʻi round trips. After Piʻilani passed away in her nursing home, Kiyoko and I were married in a simple ceremony in the chambers of a justice of Hawaʻi's Supreme Court. Soon afterwards Kiyoko received permanent residence status in the United States. Kiyoko has adapted well to Hawaiʻi, its aloha spirit, and its beautiful environment, enjoying our Maunawili home on a quiet circle nestled in a valley beneath the peak of the towering Olomana mountain. Our home became a haven for Kiyoko and an outlet for her artistic and culinary talents.

Conscious of the importance of improving her English, she attended an adult English language program for foreigners, where she made many international friends who continue to be part of her social circle. She became adept at Hawaiian quilting and has produced many decorative hangings, cushions, and bedspreads. She later added ceramics to her skills, producing attractive bowls and platters. Her art contributes to the ambiance of our home, creating an attractive environment for relaxed Hawaiian living and entertaining.

A BOOK DISCUSSION GROUP

My affiliation with the East-West Center does not require daily presence at the center. I spend considerable time reading and writing in my comfortable study at home, surrounded by books, journals, and files, benefiting from access to e-mail and the internet. Books have always played an essential and enriching role in my life, particularly through an affiliation over several decades with a book discussion group, named after my good friend Frank Damon, who launched it in the 1950s after he had concluded his university and legal studies and returned to his native Hawaiʻi to practice law. At first the group consisted of male professionals from various fields reading and discussing books dealing with a wide range of topics and representing a stimulating springboard for discussion. It now includes women and several authors.

We take turns in the selection of a book for discussion, chosen for its interest and topicality, ranging in genre from classical to modern, fiction to non-fiction, and even poetry and drama. We meet in each others' homes about once in six weeks, discussing the book of choice.

Occasionally if he or she lives in Hawai'i or is visiting, the book's author will be invited to join the meeting and add a special dimension to our discussion. George Ariyoshi, a former governor of Hawai'i, joined our group when we discussed his autobiography. At times our book discussions have taken place on weekends on neighbor islands, where we would stay at a hotel and combine the

Members of the Damon Book Discussion Group aboard a ferry to Moorea, Tahiti in 1990. Crouching in front: Ricky Reppun, Kitty Damon. Back row: Chip Higgins, Dita Ramler, Cobey Black, Beadie Dawson, consultant Yoshi Sinoto, Frank Damon (rear), the author, and Don Dawson.

evening's discussion with relaxation and recreation during the day. On one occasion, under my guidance, members traveled to Tahiti and its neighbor islands for an exploration of French Polynesia. Remarkably we have continued to meet without interruption for five decades. Some members of the group have passed away and in several cases their sons have continued their membership. The social bonding among members and the intellectual stimulation arising from the discussions have become a treasured part of our lives in Hawai'i.

THE WORLD ASSOCIATION
OF INTERNATIONAL STUDIES

I belong to a wider discussion circle named the World Association of International Studies (WAIS). This group, operating by e-mail postings, was begun by the late Stanford professor Ronald Hilton, and now continues under the editorship of a successor. The association consists of international members in various professions, linked by the internet, many with backgrounds in academia and past or present ties to Stanford. The members contribute opinions and commentary on a range of topics, often from widely different points of a philosophical, political, or social spectrum. I occasionally contribute with comments or reply to points of view raised by members. Conferences have convened at Stanford, where members could move our discussions from cyberspace to personal space.

REFLECTION ON SPORTS

I have never been a strong fan of competitive team sports, which have a pervasive impact on American culture. I prefer such individual athletic pursuits as running, swimming, and hiking. When I first joined the Punahou School faculty, shortly after arriving from Europe, I was amazed by the frenzy which surrounded the football season and the rivalry with other schools.

I was told that such competition was healthy and builds character, that it is an outlet for youthful energy, but I am not convinced that the cheerleaders' shouts of "kill them, smash them" and similar invectives represent sportsmanship, let alone build character.

I was not particularly active in athletics until about thirty years ago, when I responded at Punahou to an invitation, perhaps a dare, to join a five mile relay run with other members of the faculty. This run, which I enjoyed, led to the challenge to train for the 26.2 mile Honolulu Marathon, which was to take place in the winter of that year. I accepted that challenge, started an early morning training program, increasing my mileage and conditioning, ran that marathon with success, and eventually completed twelve additional marathons.

I soon realized that the regimen of training several times a week, varying

Crossing the finish line.

long and short training runs, had beneficial results: increased stamina and vitality, good appetite, restful sleep, and a general sense of well being. In addition, there was the camaraderie of running with friends, usually very early in the morning and often on weekends covering longer distances. However, I also enjoyed long solitary runs, which served as an opportunity for private reflection, for a kind of meditation. Interestingly, when dealing with challenges in my professional or personal life, I found that such long runs tended to act as welcome problem-solvers.

My professional duties require frequent travel for the preparation and conduct of educational projects in many parts of the world, particularly in the Asia-Pacific region. My suitcase for such trips always includes running gear. When I head for a wintry climate, I pack sweaters, long training pants, gloves and a warm cap, ready for any temperature. Regardless of the time zone, I set my alarm or request a wake-up call at my hotel for an early morning run before breakfast. I found that this routine reduces jet lag and keeps me alert for meetings and activities.

In a city abroad, whether in Asia or Europe, I run at a moderate pace, stopping when I come to an interesting spot. Sometimes I consult a city map to chart a course to a particular site. More often I run at random, discovering areas with special characteristics or architecture. At times I come across an outdoor market where I join the locals in checking the wares for sale. Early in the morning in China, in parks and squares, I encounter groups practicing *tai-chi*. Often I stop, observe for a while, and join the group in their movements, provoking good humored laughs.

Those early morning runs abroad have become a special and enjoyable form of sightseeing, a way of joining a city as it wakes in the morning.

The author with Hawai'i attorney Donald Low running up the steep incline of the Great Wall of China. Donald Low was a parent chaperone accompanying a 1979 student trip to China.

CONCLUSION

As I reflect on the progression of my life's journey, from its beginnings as a child in Vienna, traveling to England with a Kindertransport, experiencing the war years in London as an adolescent and young man, followed by a unique postwar role in Germany as interpreter at the Nuremberg trials, then leading me to the Hawaiian islands and to a career in international education, I sense a thread throughout these often turbulent times. My journey took place with the backdrop of extraordinary events on the international scene through much of the 20th century, placing me in Vienna, London, and Nuremberg as both observer and participant, and later in Hawai'i opening opportunities and challenges in education.

Living independently during the London years taught me to become resourceful, to cope with wartime conditions, to achieve bilingual English-German competence, and to acquire skills to meet the challenges facing me later in my tasks at the Nuremberg trials.

Unlike a normal sequence in normal times of uninterrupted education from early schooling to university, my educational process reflects a mixture of formal and experiential learning, supplemented and enriched by independent readings and encounters with mentors and friends who contributed to my growth.

Coping with challenges in London and Nuremberg played a far greater role in my growth than formal schooling. Meeting inspiring individuals also left enduring marks on me throughout my journey.

Conversations with two personalities come to mind. In 1946 in Rome I called on George Santayana, the philosopher, novelist, and cultural critic, who was spending the last decade of his life in a Roman convent. More than the specific content of the conversation, I recall the impact of a brilliant mind and an engaging personality. George Santayana epitomizes the stimulating insight and reflection I found over the years in meetings and conversations with others.

A later encounter in Nuremberg resonates strongly. At the trial of Nazi medical doctors accused of doing forced experiments on camp inmates, I met Wing Commander John Thompson, a British physiologist who played a key role in the investigation and evaluation of Nazi medical experiments. A medical graduate of the University of Edinburgh. Dr. Thompson had expertise in high altitude experimentation and psychiatry, and had done extensive research on issues surrounding medical experimentation. I recall many long conversations with him on medical ethics and the limits of medical intervention and research. He also discussed his philosophy of education, drawing on his experience as a medical educator teaching anatomy. He talked of taking his students on field studies, leading them to observe the performance of athletes in their uses of the body. He understood that beyond the classroom, students could gain enhanced insights into human anatomy. Such examples of non-traditional teaching and experiential learning impressed me greatly, and helped me to develop an inquiring mind and a strong attraction to teaching.

There is no doubt that the Nuremberg experience had a powerful impact on my life, on my world view, and on my later role as educator and communicator. Facing the former leaders of Nazi Germany, both during pretrial interrogations and in the courtroom, stripped of their position and power, I saw them as ordinary individuals, characterizing what has been described by the philosopher Hannah Arendt as "the banality of evil." In Nuremberg I learned, through witnesses, testimony, and documents, of man's inhumanity to man on a massive scale and the consequences of a brutal dictatorship.

On a personal and family level, with the arduous flight of my parents from Austria and the arrest and killing of a grandparent, that inhumanity resonated directly and deeply. The Nuremberg experience, indeed the history of the Nazi era in the 1930s, convinced me of the danger of unchecked power and of the need for a global rule of law.

In Hawai'i, when an invitation to teach foreign languages was extended by Punahou School, I discovered the challenge of reaching out to young minds and the satisfaction of contributing to their growth. My later responsibilities for coordination of curriculum and faculty development gave me an opportunity to collaborate with colleagues to improve the quality of learning and teaching.

Casting a wider net, by establishing the Wo Center at Punahou, I found it possible to create an international educational base serving Punahou and the Hawai'i community. This center continues to offer opportunities for international study programs to students from Hawai'i and, reciprocally, to welcome students from many countries around the globe. Offerings have now expanded to include faculty development programs, both for Punahou teachers and for faculty invited from various countries in the Asia-Pacific region.

In a sense, the Wo Center represents the flowering of a seed planted decades ago when I started teaching foreign languages at Punahou School.

Similarly, my current position as Adjunct Fellow with the education programs of Hawai'i's East-West Center represents an extension of my decades of commitment to international education, allowing me to contribute to the East-West Center's educational outreach to the Asia-Pacific region, both for Asian and U.S. faculties and for American and international students. As a special personal reward, my efforts in international education have yielded strong bonds of friendship with colleagues in many parts of the world and have introduced me to the variety and richness of world cultures through travel and experience.

After experiencing upheavals in the 20th century and after participating in the Nuremberg trials, my life in Hawai'i has offered welcome contrasts: a harmonious setting in a multiethnic society, an

With Hawai'i-born sumotori Akebono (Chad Rowan) in 1999. Akebono was the first foreign wrestler to attain *Yokozuna,* the sport's highest rank.

attractive physical environment, a close network of family and friends, and an excellent base for outreach to the Asia-Pacific region.

In summing up events and experiences over the years, I am convinced that in facing 21st century challenges to global peace and survival, education represents the most important element in our quest for a harmonious world. I feel blessed that in a small way I have been given opportunities to contribute to this mission.

ACKNOWLEDGMENTS

AUTHOR'S ACKNOWLEDGMENTS

For several years friends and colleagues have encouraged me to write and share impressions and feelings as I look back to eight decades of a life span, a journey which took me from early turbulent years in Europe to a career in education in Hawai'i. Writing about myself required a leap in expression. From my writing background of articles with professional themes, at some distance from subjective feelings, this memoir compelled me to open and probe memories of personal and public events I had not previously shared. It was not an easy process, and I could not have achieved the memoir without the encouragement and professional assistance of friends and associates.

Among the friends who have urged me for years to write about my life are Elaine Blitman, a close colleague at Punahou School, now retired, who gently prodded me to put finger to keyboard and start the process. Another close friend, Mark Goldberg, author and editor on educational themes and fellow Fulbright scholar, offered encouragement and helpful suggestions.

Paul (Doc) Berry, editor of this volume, served for several decades as teacher and academic leader at Punahou School. As a colleague who took an interest in my story, his contributions as an experienced author, editor and stylist went far beyond the sculpting and sharpening of prose. He urged me to probe more deeply and explore more widely the events and issues raised in this memoir. He generously offered his time and contributed critiques which were always well founded and to the point.

My deep appreciation goes to MacKinnon Simpson, historian and book designer, who enriched this memoir with skillful layout and placement of photographs. His remarkable research led to the uncovering of photos and illustrations which form the backdrop to my story and enliven its presentation for the reader. And warm thanks to my daughter Dita Ramler, a dedicated librarian, who provided valuable advice.

DESIGNER'S ACKNOWLEDGMENTS

First and foremost to Sig, not just for the manuscript of his incredible life story, but also for saving all those pictures over all that time! And to his daughter Dita, Librarian at Punahou School's Bishop Learning Center, for her careful proofing and her suggestions, all of which made this a better book. Doc Berry, writer and editor extraordinaire, meticulously shaped Sig's manuscript, and later provided me both with inestimable help in captioning the images and encouragement critiquing the layout. Kylee Omo, Punahou School's Archivist, was a great help in sourcing Punahou images of Sig's long career there.

Ross Togashi manages the Map Collection at UH's Hamilton Library and, as he has done in several prior books, located THE perfect map to illustrate the escape routes from the Nazis of Sig to London and his parents to Palestine. But how to determine the

Keio students at work in a Punahou classroom.

precise routes? A Google search, of course. That netted a pair of European train historians: Thorsten Büker, of Cologne, Germany and Boris Chomenko, of Mulhouse, France. They researched the routes using 1940 rail maps and timetables and then created the routes on the map the Ross had provided.

Another source discovered via Google was prolific German author Peter Heigl, creator of a number of lavishly illustrated books on wartime and post-war Germany. He provided me with some great images I could not find elsewhere, sent us a number of his books, and corresponded at length with Sig.

Book projects are complex animals, and I confess to having a secret source of help—Mark and Keith Fujimoto, and David Wilson, at the University branch of Professional Image on King Street in Moʻiliʻili. Mark is a true Macintosh and InDesign guru, always willing to help make something better, to go the extra mile. This shop is what K•nko's should have been. THANKS!

Several esteemed members of my Princeton Writer's List stepped forward with help, especially Jim Lewis, Eric Lubell, Helen Michaud, David Paul and Steve Wilson. Karl Brehmer, Charles Buckley, and Sabine Eiche offered translations of various wartime German phrases such as labels and signs.

Sig's Kindertransport experience of leaving his family and starting anew in London at 14 was life-changing. I would like to thank Robert Sugar, creator of the Kindertransport exhibit, Kindertransport Association President, Kurt Goldberger, and Lilian Levy at the Jewish Refugees Committee in London who all offered their help. Lilian even found several of Sig's original Kindertransport documents!

Frank Meisler was a fellow Kindertransport child who later became a famed sculptor in Tel Aviv. He graciously allowed us to use an image of his installation in London's Liverpool railroad station. Thanks to Hanita Tovi and Malka Fulman at his gallery in Tel Aviv.

Dennis Weidner runs a fascinating website called Historical Clothing: http://histclo.com/ but which is far more than that, with concise histories and photos of the Anschluss among other events. Dennis was extremely helpful in directing me to image sources.

Nancy Hartman, in the photo archives at the United States Holocaust Memorial Museum (USHMM) helped immensely in sourcing and providing images. Per our agreement with USHMM, we are including here the following disclaimer: "The views or opinions expressed in this book, and the context in which the images are used, do not necessarily reflect the views or policy of, nor imply approval or endorsement by the United States Holocaust Memorial Museum."

Both the USHMM and the Library of Congress use third-party photo houses to duplicate their images. Victor Pulupa at Dodge Color could not have been more helpful in getting me the scans quickly. Erica Kelly at the Library of Congress coordinated our order for both images and scans.

Geoff Walden is the creator of the Third Reich website: http://www.thirdreichruins.com and was extremely helpful in helping me source images.

Palolo artist Lee Samson took an extremely faded color photo of Annie and Moses Ahuna in front of their Hilo home and created, or perhaps re-created, a photo that looks like it just arrived from Kodak.

As always, the Macintosh community, especially the HMAUS List, was willing to answer technical questions posed at any hour of the day and night. Thanks to Michael Blasco, Bill Fuller, Doug Frick, Marcie Katz, Joan Matsukawa, Rolf Nordahl, and Terrence Young. Linda Butts gave me some valuable lessons in InDesign and helped me over a rough patch in converting files.

Finally, to Lori Ikehara-Lyman who provided her camera, encouragement, and a trained artistic eye throughout.